THE RATIONALE OF THE STERLING AREA

THE RATIONALE OF
THE STERLING AREA

Texts and Commentary

BY

A. R. CONAN

LONDON
MACMILLAN & CO LTD
NEW YORK · ST MARTIN'S PRESS
1961

Copyright © A. R. Conan, 1961

MACMILLAN AND COMPANY LIMITED
London Bombay Calcutta Madras Melbourne

THE MACMILLAN COMPANY OF CANADA LIMITED
Toronto

ST MARTIN'S PRESS INC
New York

PRINTED IN GREAT BRITAIN

PREFACE

THE title of this work implies an obligation to examine certain basic issues significant for the sterling system: the work itself comprises selected texts referring to these issues, with a critical commentary prefixed as an introduction. Most of the texts have been taken from the evidence submitted to the Radcliffe Committee or from its Report but some supplementary material from other sources has been included. Part of the oral evidence tendered to the Committee has been utilised in the introduction.

The main texts studied are two memoranda prepared by the Treasury: one is a factual paper which discusses the origins and present operation of the system and deals with recent history in terms of the impact on the United Kingdom's external reserves and liabilities; the other describes the conditions which govern the formation of policy and considers the effect of monetary measures on the balance of payments. Included also are extracts from the memoranda submitted by the central banks of overseas sterling countries; two papers on the sterling balances; an official statement of United Kingdom policy on the sterling area; and extracts from the Radcliffe Committee's Report dealing with certain aspects of policy. An appendix has been added with (unofficial) estimates of the United Kingdom's overseas assets and liabilities.

The extracts from the evidence submitted to the Radcliffe Committee, and the CSO paper on the sterling balances, are reproduced by permission of the Controller of HM Stationery Office. Acknowledgment is due also to *The Times* and the *Westminster Bank Review* for permission to reprint material which originally appeared in those journals.

CONTENTS

INTRODUCTION

(i) *Elements of the Problem*

A REALISTIC study of the issues with which this book is concerned must be based on a survey of the structure and working of the sterling system. The Treasury paper reproduced on pp. 33–47, which purports to give such a survey, should first be examined.

The paper begins with a reference to the origins of the sterling area, notes recent developments, and avers that the fundamental structure of the system remains little changed. It shows that the factors which together determine the strength of sterling are complex but ultimately find expression in the relationship between reserves and liabilities. The elements in this relationship are then distinguished.

Four factors come under discussion: the United Kingdom current balance; the R.S.A. current balance; long-term investment overseas; and the sterling holdings of non-sterling countries. Only the first and third of these can be regarded as 'internal' i.e. dependent primarily on United Kingdom policy; the others are external in that they are a result of policies and decisions elsewhere. The distinction is relevant since the internal factors affect the size of the gap between reserves and liabilities while the external factors do not.

A summary of the results is given in the following passage:

> The picture which emerges is that, in present circumstances a current account surplus in the United Kingdom balance of payments is of fundamental importance to the whole strength and soundness of sterling, though it does not in itself ensure either a reduction of the sterling balances or an increase in the reserves. Overseas investment (which is natural and beneficial to us and the recipients and with which the normal current account surplus is largely bound up) works against a reduction of the sterling balances; and the withdrawal of sterling balances held by the N.S.A. will, so long as it continues, work against an increase in the reserves—all this in spite of a substantial United Kingdom current

surplus in most years. In short, it is only when we have a surplus on current account greater than our net investment overseas that we are able to improve our external monetary position (whether by reducing the total of the sterling balances'or by increasing the reserves).

This statement relates to the United Kingdom. If the problem be considered in a wider context the analysis can be regarded as incomplete since it omits the contribution of the overseas sterling area: although a non-sterling surplus in that sector increases the sterling balances as well as the central reserves, the process raises the international liquidity ratio as such balances are merely liabilities between two member countries. A full statement should therefore take account of the diverse factors operating throughout the system.

In any case, as the memorandum itself implies, a more searching study is needed for a true appreciation. 'The problem is not merely one of increasing the size of the sterling area reserves. In the final analysis it will depend rather on the capacity of the sterling area as a whole to achieve and maintain a sufficiently strong balance of payments position with the rest of the world.' An attempt must now be made to examine the problem along these lines.

(ii) *Determinants of the Reserves*

The validity of the analysis in the Treasury memorandum may be tested by reference to recent trends in the working of the sterling system. For the present purpose it is convenient to take separately the factors operating on the reserves and those which occasion changes in liabilities. In this section the former will be considered.

The fundamental factors can be isolated by examining the sterling area balance of payments with the non-sterling world, which is the resultant of forces operating in both the United Kingdom and the overseas sterling area. A statement of the outturn for the years 1950–59 is on p. 3.

A study of the data will reveal major structural changes. Formerly the working of the system in relation to the non-sterling world depended on certain reciprocal links between the

United Kingdom and the rest of the sterling area: in particular
the deficit of the former was set against the surplus earned by the
latter. The current account proves that latterly the system has
been unable to function in this way since the overseas sterling
area has not earned a surplus.

Sterling Area Transactions with non-Sterling World

(£ million)

	U.K. Current Balance	R.S.A. Current Balance[1]	Total	R.S.A. Gold Output	R.S.A. Capital Inflow
1950	14	247	261	179	121
1951	—739	—11	—750	178	176
1952	—121	—146	—267	183	257
1953	27	68	95	185	151
1954	—56	—116	—172	203	152
1955	—287	—169	—456	217	136
1956	—64	—217	—281	233	157
1957	—131	—410	—541	249	141
1958	—89	—561	—650	257	374
1959	—84	—224	—308	289	315

[1] Excluding gold but including grants.

SOURCE: *U.K. Balance of Payments, 1946–57* (H.M.S.O., 1959);
Cmnd. 1188. Gold figures from IMF.

A detailed break-down of the data would show more clearly
the conditions under which the system now operates. The
R.S.A. has an adverse balance not merely for trade but also for
invisibles: on an earnings basis the deficit is in fact far greater
than the figures given in the table since these include grants,
which in recent years have been of the order of £100 million
per annum. Moreover, even when gold is added, it does not
balance the account. In 1957–58 the current deficit was as
much as £400–500 million per annum, which could be offset to
the extent of about £250 million by gold: for 1959 there was an
apparent surplus with gold included but only after taking
credit for grants.

To some extent the deficit is the counterpart of capital
receipts and may be regarded as innocuous in so far as it
represents imports needed for projects financed by external

capital. But there is evidence that such an assessment is incomplete and that the deficit may primarily be attributable to a level of investment higher than can be financed by resources currently available: in such circumstances external capital is needed also to cover the balance of payments gap created by this disparity. Such a view seems to be confirmed by the exceptionally large figures for capital imports during 1958 since in that year both India and New Zealand were forced to have recourse to 'distress' borrowing when overseas reserves were seriously depleted.

The analysis brings out the vital function of two factors in the balance of payments: gold and capital imports. Some further comment on each may help to elucidate their significance.

The first of these factors clearly becomes of special significance if the overseas sterling area does not contribute to the central reserves from trade earnings. In the past the gold output of South Africa and other sterling countries supplemented the surplus on visible trade with the non-sterling world: the whole of the output was available for this purpose as there were no considerable transactions on invisible account. Now the situation is more complex in that gold has manifold functions: as far as possible it must cover the adverse balance on trade account while it is needed also to meet the deficit on invisibles. Only after providing for these commitments can the residue (if any) be used to set against the United Kingdom non-sterling deficit or to fortify the central reserves.

During recent years it has not been possible for gold to fulfil these several functions. This result cannot be attributed to supply conditions, which in fact have been exceptionally favourable. In the first place, production has shown a large expansion, primarily from new mines in South Africa, the total rising by as much as 50 per cent within a very few years: in absolute terms the yield increased from an annual average of £180 million for 1950–52 to over £280 million in 1959. Secondly, the United Kingdom has been able to secure a higher proportion of the output. For several years after 1950 the central reserves received less than £100 million per annum, with an annual average of only £75 million for 1951–52. There was, however, a sharp increase when the London gold market was re-opened in 1954 and the free market premium disappeared. The whole South African output then came to London and as a result the reserves received as much as £150 million in 1954–55 and over £220 million in 1956–59.

The inflow into the reserves perhaps calls for explanation since, on a strict accounting basis, the entire output of the sterling area has latterly been absorbed by the R.S.A. current deficit. Reference to the balance of payments statement will show how the mechanism has worked: the reserves have received newly-mined gold only because, by substitution, receipts of non-sterling capital can be set against the deficit.

The gold factor can now be evaluated. It is apparent that the level of the central reserves has been largely governed by the expansion in South Africa's gold output and the arrangements for its sale: in other words the increase in supplies was occasioned by technical rather than economic forces. An assessment of the future should accordingly take account of the estimate that output in the Union may not rise much above current levels and may begin to decline within the next ten years. Moreover, even apart from the possibility of sales elsewhere than in London, little scope exists for obtaining additional supplies from current production as nearly the whole of the output is now channelled into the central reserves: there is here a contrast with the situation a few years ago when less than half the total was shipped to London. In addition it should be noted that the South African gold lodged in the reserves is not earned by United Kingdom exports but is bought with sterling carrying a gold guarantee: as a result the gold is under earmark for the Union so long as the sterling is unspent.

It is also apparent that a certain complementary relationship subsists between the gold factor and the import of capital. The flow of newly-mined gold from the overseas sterling area to London has long been a feature of the sterling system; the replenishment of the reserves from capital receipts is a novel development. Before the war the United Kingdom (which did not then import capital) supplied virtually all the capital needs of other sterling countries; latterly, however, these countries (as well as the United Kingdom) have drawn heavily on non-sterling capital. In fact, this capital, not gold, has become the major determinant of the reserves.

The trend is noteworthy because an increase in the reserves derived from a capital inflow is not the same as an increase earned by trade. In the first place capital flows are characteristically unstable and liable to interruption. Secondly, the process creates at least a contingent liability as the capital may be repatriated. Finally, there is not merely a contingent but an actual liability in respect of the return payable on the capital received.

Two points should be emphasised. One is the magnitude of the inflow. In the ten years 1950–59 the United Kingdom absorbed almost £1,000 million of non-sterling capital and the overseas sterling area some £2,000 million. The service of the investment represented by these funds necessarily involves heavy commitments payable in non-sterling currency. The burden is already evident in the amount which the sterling area now has to transfer to the United States as interest and dividends: in 1959 the debit was $600 million as compared with only $300 million in 1951.

The character of the capital is relevant also. In the case of the overseas sterling area much of it (about £1,000 million) has been on public account, nearly all from government or institutional sources rather than from issues on international money markets. It seems likely that where finance is derived from official sources, the flow may tend to be discontinuous since it depends on political rather than economic factors; in addition, repayment obligations will be exceptionally onerous as refinancing of such loans is rarely practicable.

These potential difficulties may be accentuated by the claims of business capital. In post-war years this category has comprised mainly direct investment, with a high proportion of retained profits. It is clear that the quasi-automatic increase implicit in reinvestment can continue until there is a very large liability on account of both capital and profits: the figures quoted above for the amount due to the United States (most of which represents the return on direct investment) exemplify the

possible rate of expansion. Here, too, any check to the capital
inflow, even through a reduction in the rate of reinvestment,
could expose the balance of payments to considerable strain.

The evidence suggests that the impact of this new force may
prove decisive. In certain respects there is a parallel with
Canada. There, as in the overseas sterling area, a high rate of
capital expenditure since the war has involved a large deficit in
the current balance associated with free use of external finance.
In both cases the figures for visible trade negative the view that
foreign investment automatically creates an increase in exports
sufficient to cover commitments. In addition, there has been a
sharp rise in the deficit on invisibles: for Canada in 1959 it was
double the 1955 figure and accounted for about three-quarters of
the total current deficit. These trends have occasioned doubts
as to whether Canada ought to expand at a rate which involves
massive investment of foreign capital, especially as under such
conditions it becomes more difficult to counter a recession imported from abroad.

Complex policy issues are here involved. Although in the
overseas sterling area as in Canada external capital is needed to
ensure rapid development, there may be a case for accepting a
slower rate of progress. Restrictions on the inflow of funds
would slacken the pace of expansion but a sudden cessation such
as might occur during a slump would cause a major dislocation.
In addition, it is as yet by no means certain that the current
balance will be able to sustain the effects of the large-scale
capital imports received since the war.

Whatever the course of future policy it seems essential to
make clear the character and extent of recent changes in the
balance of payments structure. The effect of these changes is to
base the system first, on the R.S.A. output of gold, and secondly,
on non-sterling capital. The Treasury memorandum fails to
take account of the results: working on the assumption that the
overseas sterling area is normally in surplus, it does not complete the analysis. More detailed study indicates that under
present conditions it may not be easy to secure a continuous
replenishment of the reserves since some degree of instability
attaches to the components of the surplus. This underlines the

need for an appraisal of the liabilities against which the reserves are held.

(iii) *The Genesis of the Sterling Balances*

The problem presented by the existence of large sterling balances originally created during the war is stated in the Treasury memorandum as follows:

> Whenever doubt is cast on our solvency these balances come under pressure, thus tending to aggravate the very situation that caused the doubts to arise. The use of sterling as an international currency makes it inevitable that we should have large overseas monetary liabilities. But it does not explain their present size, which derives from economic developments in the war and post-war years and has little to do with the normal requirements of a centre for international finance.

A paper on the sterling balances prepared by the Central Statistical Office is reproduced on pp. 48–62. It can be read with the paper submitted by the Bank of England to the Radcliffe Committee, which is on pp. 62–67.

The C.S.O. paper purports to give a technical and historical account of the figures. It notes that at the end of the war a large proportion of the balances represented obligations to other countries arising from wartime exigencies rather than the working balances or normal reserves voluntarily held in London. The increase in the holdings of the colonial territories since the war is attributed to the expansion of colonial economies at a time of rising prices, with the comment that in recent years a large capital inflow has offset the deficit on current account. It is pointed out that as the coverage of the figures for the sterling balances is much wider than that of the figures for the reserves, the absolute difference between the two shows an unduly adverse balance of net indebtedness.

The Bank of England paper considers briefly the nature of the balances. It classes them as primarily liquid resources held against local currency issues overseas or against future liabilities to be discharged in sterling: there is here perhaps some difference of emphasis with the C.S.O. paper which states that 'a substantial part is held for long-term purposes and can legiti-

mately be regarded as permanent or semi-permanent investment in the United Kingdom'. The Bank then reviews
fluctuations in the amounts held by different groups of
countries. In the course of this review it is noted that while the
total for the balances had changed little in post-war years, the
composition of the total had altered very considerably: the
holdings of non-sterling countries have fallen heavily but there
has been an increase in the holdings of sterling countries.

Neither paper includes a statistical analysis of the factors
operating on sterling balances since the war and although they
are mentioned in the Treasury memorandum, the treatment
lacks precision. Detailed analysis is, however, needed to expose
the problem and must therefore be effected here. It will be confined to the holdings of sterling countries and will show that
since the war the character of these liabilities has been transformed.

Three factors have been of primary importance in this process
and it is essential for the demonstration not only to specify them
but also to indicate their magnitude.

The first factor is the favourable balance (current account)
of the United Kingdom with the rest of the sterling area: this by
itself absorbs an equivalent amount of sterling held by countries
in deficit with the United Kingdom. The cumulative surplus
from 1946 to 1959 amounted to £3,500 million: since R.S.A.
balances at the end of the war were only £2,400 million, it is
clear that the surplus operating alone would have liquidated the
total.

On the other hand purchases of gold from the overseas
sterling area have been substantial: as the United Kingdom
pays in sterling these transactions create *new* balances. During
the years 1946–59 gold purchases totalled £1,800 million and
sterling to an equivalent amount was accordingly credited to
the accounts of the countries concerned.

An even more important factor which occasioned the creation
of new liabilities was the outflow of capital from the United
Kingdom to the overseas sterling area: this outflow, which since
the war has exceeded £2,500 million, further replenished the
balances of sterling countries.

B

A fully comprehensive statement would include other factors also but would not alter the main outlines of the picture: the R.S.A. deficit with non-sterling countries, for example, could be approximately offset against receipts of non-sterling capital. The data summarised above should therefore be sufficient to show that while the accounting total of the R.S.A. balances is nearly the same as in 1945, the true position is essentially different. At the end of the war the total represented debts incurred for war purposes: these have been repaid. In their place are new liabilities fully covered by assets such as gold and overseas investment.

The results of the analysis can be verified by detailed examination of the data for individual countries or groups of countries. The wartime accumulation of sterling was largely due to heavy military expenditure in Egypt and (undivided) India: at the end of the war these countries owned balances to a total of approximately £1,500 million but by 1958 over £1,000 million had been repaid. On the other hand the balances of the Colonies and the Middle East oil countries were not unduly large at the end of the war but thereafter rose rapidly: the increase in the former case was nearly £900 million between 1945 and 1958 while in the latter case the total rose from £70 million in 1950 to nearly £350 million in 1956. At the end of 1958 these two groups probably accounted for almost two-thirds of the balances held by sterling countries.

The figures corroborate the evidence already cited. In the first place they demonstrate by concrete instances that the wartime balances have to a great extent been repaid. (More evidence on this point could be presented by reviewing the payments problems which have arisen since the war in countries such as Australia and New Zealand: in both cases London balances have at times fallen so low as to necessitate corrective measures, and the same is true of several other sterling countries.) Secondly, the data for the Colonies and the Middle East can be utilised to account for the existing balances. In the latter case the increase may reasonably be ascribed to heavy investment by the oil industry, although details are lacking.

For the Colonies official estimates permit of a more precise statement. It will be found that the post-war additions to these holdings were in no sense earned since the cumulative total for the current balance of payments shows a deficit: to set against this deficit, however, there were capital receipts (Government loans, grants and business capital) which exceeded £1,000 million.

On a longer-term view it can be seen that the process described is in no way unusual but typifies the normal working of the sterling system. The United Kingdom surplus with other sterling countries has been offset in part by sales of newly-mined gold: at the same time the United Kingdom has, as in the past, functioned as the major source of capital for the overseas sterling area. If the final outcome has been the maintenance of sterling balances at a high level, that cannot be imputed to defects in the mechanism: had the end-war balances been scaled down (as contemplated in the Anglo-American Agreement of 1945) the surplus with the overseas sterling area would have largely neutralised the creation of balances through gold sales and capital flows. In fact the system was over-loaded and was thus unable to digest both the wartime and the post-war balances. Only in this sense can the present total be regarded as a legacy of the war.

Once the true character of the existing sterling balances has been established it is impermissible to regard them as comparable to war debts or to assess the burden involved without taking into account the assets held against them. In other words a distinction must be made between liabilities which are fully covered by assets and those which are not. The balances of sterling countries are liabilities just as a bank's deposits are liabilities and were in fact created in much the same way: the parallel is not invalidated simply because only part of the assets (gold) normally appears on the credit side, the remainder (overseas investments) being omitted from the reckoning. The very inadequate presentation does, however, suggest that the usual form of the ratio between reserves and liabilities may need to be recast if it is to be taken as an index of solvency. This point must now be examined.

(iv) *The Reserve Ratio*

In evidence before the Radcliffe Committee the Treasury placed much emphasis on the relationship between reserves and liabilities, stating that the main policy objective was to secure an improvement in this relationship. If the ratio (in some form or other) is to be regarded as crucial in the working of the sterling system there should clearly be an acceptable definition of its scope and adequate data on the component items. At present these requirements are not met.

The problem is usually discussed in the terms appropriate to conventional banking practice, reserves being taken as the United Kingdom's holdings of gold and convertible currencies (the central reserves) and liabilities as the sterling balances. Apart altogether from the critique elaborated in the preceding section, there are grounds on which it could be maintained that such an interpretation is open to objection.

A preliminary point may first be mentioned: it is rarely clear whether the ratio refers to the United Kingdom or to the sterling area. If the latter is intended it would be appropriate to treat the entire system as a currency region and therefore to count against international reserves only such liabilities as are due to non-sterling countries: on this basis the Radcliffe Committee noted that a reduction in the sterling balances would do little to increase the liquidity of the system as a whole although it would improve the position of the United Kingdom. Moreover, on the same basis a full statement would take account of international assets held by countries other than the United Kingdom, especially as in recent years the central reserves have been drawn upon by certain sterling countries in order to build up their own reserves. Although these are not normally utilised to cover exchange needs, they may be regarded as a kind of supplementary reserve and can on occasion be activated: in 1956, for example, Australia made available to the United Kingdom £A25 million of gold from domestic stocks and when New Zealand ran into payments difficulties in 1958 its gold was pledged as security for a dollar loan.

With such adjustments the ratio of assets to liabilities would look very different from that normally shown. But even when the usual statement of the ratio as referring to the United Kingdom alone is accepted, the presentation can be criticised on several grounds.

One objection to the normal form of the ratio is that it suggests unrealistic contingencies. On any reasonable basis it is unnecessary to hold *international* reserves to meet all withdrawals since the balances will to a considerable extent be utilised for payments to the United Kingdom. It seems equally unnecessary to provide against large-scale withdrawals as most countries do not now hold much more sterling than they need. Least of all is it necessary to envisage the repayment of the total since much of it is held for long-term purposes. There is moreover little support for the view that the balances are exceptionally volatile: in evidence before the Radcliffe Committee the Governor of the Bank of England conceded that they were 'not particularly hot' and had proved to be fairly stable on the whole. Liabilities of this kind do not need to be backed £ for £ by *liquid* resources, which are appropriate only for that proportion of the total likely to be withdrawn at short notice. It can therefore be maintained that the canons of sound banking practice should not require a very high proportion of the assets held against such liabilities to be in the form of gold and dollars.

Another objection is that the figures for the sterling balances are themselves misleading. The Radcliffe Committee revealed that the total as officially computed does not represent a net liability since the balances are shown gross and include items to which there are counterparts in the form of liabilities to the United Kingdom. The Committee expressed the view that if these counterclaims were taken into account the net total would be much lower than that now published.

There is a further qualification to be made before the figures can be accepted. Detailed analysis of the holdings of the Colonies discloses that this category in particular over-states very considerably the extent of the liabilities which can properly be regarded as external: it comprises a number of different elements and although the term 'colonial sterling balances' is used to cover all assets held in London on colonial account, these assets are in fact to a large extent owned by the United Kingdom and not by colonial residents. The qualification applies specially to the items which make up the greater part of the total viz. banking funds and currency reserves. In both cases the balances are to a very great extent liabilities only in name since the sterling used as currency backing comes from the London offices of banks (generally British-owned) with branches in the Colonies while the banking funds are the London accounts of such branches.

These defects limit the usefulness of the figures as a measure of the external liabilities of the United Kingdom and thus impair the validity of the reserve ratio. Its validity is further impaired by the fact that the conventional presentation of the ratio understates the asset total as only part (gold) normally appears on the credit side, the remainder (overseas investments) being omitted. The omission seems to be unjustifiable since most of the liabilities arose from capital exports and ordinary banking practice naturally requires the corresponding assets to be shown against them.

A more rational presentation would involve a statement with full coverage of the main items. Within this general framework the liquidity ratio must be fixed as a matter of practical judgment: no bank holds all its assets in liquid form and if it is unrealistic to regard the whole of the sterling balances as highly liquid or fully expendable, long-term assets may properly be included. Moreover, although overseas investments are not immediately realisable, it has been found in two world wars that they can be mobilised to augment the reserves. Nor are such operations necessarily confined to wartime emergencies: in 1956, for example, dollar securities were pledged as security for a loan in the United States while in the same year the sale of a single concern (the Trinidad Oil Company) replenished the central reserves to the extent of nearly $200 million.

The evidence makes it clear that neither the liquidity nor the solvency of the United Kingdom as the banker of the sterling area should be assessed on the basis of the crude relationship between the sterling balances and the central reserves. The true position can be ascertained only by listing all the main categories of overseas assets and liabilities in such a way that they can be summed to yield a net credit or debit. No official census of this kind has yet been taken but an attempt at an estimate along these lines is given in the Appendix. The results suggest that the United Kingdom has regained its status as a creditor country, with a net surplus perhaps not far below the pre-war level.

(v) *The Foundations of Policy*

In preceding sections it has been evident that the complex structure of the sterling area controls the working of the system. The same characteristic applies in the policy field. Although no detailed programme is normally laid down for the whole sterling area, the United Kingdom, as the centre of the system, has special responsibilities in formulating policy since its decisions may affect other sterling countries. Conversely, events in these countries may react on the United Kingdom, which has then to make appropriate adjustments in policy.

Some aspects of the problem are discussed in the Treasury memorandum on Monetary Policy and External Economic Problems (pp. 68–85). The memorandum notes that United Kingdom policy must be framed with due regard to certain conditions which limit freedom of action in this field: those specified are the status of sterling as an international currency; the need for long-term investment overseas; and the existing reserve ratio. The conclusion is that in such an environment the dominant policy objectives should be the maintenance of confidence in sterling and the creation of an adequate external surplus.

The first of these objectives is stated to be essential because of the unfavourable reserve ratio: weakness here implies that a failure of confidence could lead to large-scale withdrawals by overseas holders of sterling as well as to repercussions on the reserve through speculative movements. Experience since the war has shown that the sterling holdings of N.S.A. countries are in fact liable to sharp fluctuations and that movements in them have occasioned large changes in the reserves. More than ten years ago the proximate cause of such fluctuations was described in the following terms:

The overseas sterling balances are probably the most persistent enemy of external confidence in sterling. Every foreign banker, merchant or politician who seeks to assess the position of sterling looks not merely at the profit and loss account—that is, at the current balance of payments—but at the balance sheet. And in the latter his eyes fasten on two items: the overseas liabilities payable on demand on the one hand, and the available cash reserve on the other. Britain's sterling liabilities, on the latest available evidence, amount to about £3,200 million; the gold and dollar reserve, even when written up in terms of devalued sterling, amounts to only about £500 million. How can there be confidence in a banker whose financial position looks as precarious as this?[1]

Although the ratio has improved since these words were written in 1949 it still seems *prima facie* highly unfavourable, with disclosed assets no more than one-third of stated liabilities. But, as shown earlier, the figures are unacceptable: when they are submitted to close scrutiny their inadequacy is revealed and the attempt to evaluate the evidence underlines the need for more detailed information on overseas assets and liabilities. Even the imperfect data now available tend to support the Radcliffe Committee's view of the advantages to be derived from firmer estimates: foremost among such advantages is the fact that confidence would be buttressed by fuller knowledge. It seems evident, therefore, that authoritative definition of the extent to which the United Kingdom has regained creditor status is long overdue.

Confidence is also an element in the second policy objective: the creation of an adequate external surplus. In this case the Treasury memorandum stated that a payments surplus was needed for several reasons: to sustain confidence, to prevent erosion of the reserves as a result of the export of capital, and to provide for some increase in them. A figure of £300–350 million was given as 'the average balance of payments surplus on current account which is desirable year-in year-out over the years immediately ahead'. Subsequently, however, Treasury witnesses told the Committee that they were inclined to assume that resources should be found for a surplus of about £450 million a

---

[1] *Economist*, 3 December 1949.

year in the early 1960s in order to make room for a larger volume of long-term investment abroad.

Here again the statistical basis on which the case was founded appears to have been defective. The target figure was assumed to be far above the outturn attained during recent years: in fact, however, the official figures for the surplus are known to be under-estimated. A properly-articulated balance of payments statement should credit the current account not merely with the income actually received from overseas investments but also with reinvested profits; a contra entry in the capital account would show such reinvestment as an outflow of capital. Since retained profits have latterly been of major importance as a source of direct investment, the exclusion of this item in whole or in part from the current account (as in the United Kingdom balance of payments) vitiates the results.

It is not at present possible to estimate with any certainty the extent to which the surplus is under-stated but the figures available for various countries suggest that the margin of error may be very large. It is quite conceivable that the surplus earned during recent years may not have been below even the higher of the two figures named in the Treasury memorandum. Should this prove true the conclusion is justified that, as in the case of the reserve ratio, confidence has been adversely affected by the failure to make provision for an adequate record of results.

If, however, policy is to be based on the assumption that the balance of payments should be strengthened, there is a choice between a number of possible alternatives. The Treasury review of policy measures was confined to brief mention of exchange control and interest rates. The former was considered to be merely an adjunct to a general economic plan and although more attention was given to monetary policy it was implied that the scope for this instrument would probably be limited: Bank Rate changes could be expected to operate on short-term capital movements mainly through the confidence factor (which was likely to outweigh interest-rate differentials) and to have some effect on capital exports. As regards the current balance the Treasury view was that monetary policy could work only indirectly and to the extent that it influenced internal economic conditions.

The Radcliffe Committee's conclusions were substantially in accord with those in the Treasury memorandum. Although Bank Rate could be used as a weapon for protecting the reserves, the Committee thought that quick results were not to be expected from the impact via total demand on the balance of trade: it noted also that an increase in the rate involved higher costs for the service of the sterling balances and would, in general, do little to attract short-term capital. The Committee were, however, prepared to accept the view that there could be a confidence effect, especially if a Bank Rate move were part of a package deal made up of several measures.

In discussion of this problem neither the Treasury nor the Committee gave much attention to the repercussions on the overseas sterling area, although the latter pointed out that high rates tended to check borrowing in London and noted that sterling balances would be run down if funds were attracted from overseas sterling countries without exchange control: on the other hand, the cost of a prolonged period of higher interest rates might work in the reverse direction.

Notwithstanding these factors, it has been found during the past few years that the repercussions of interest rate changes on the overseas sterling area have been quite considerable. The effect on capital exports is perhaps somewhat limited since the major part of this flow now comprises direct investment, which would be rather insensitive to such measures: to that extent the impact is lessened. Furthermore, the reduction in sterling balances occasioned by transfers of funds to London can in part be offset by the accrued interest: between 1950 and 1956 the net increase was estimated at over £80 million per annum. It has not always been possible, however, to disregard the trend of rates in London and the monetary authorities in overseas sterling countries have sometimes found it necessary to raise their own rates. Where this occurred it tended to weaken United Kingdom policy as transfers to London would be checked but the higher interest rates no doubt had some effect in damping down inflation and thus supported monetary measures at the centre.

Reference to the impact will be found in several of the

memoranda submitted to the Radcliffe Committee by the central banks of overseas sterling countries. Both Australia and New Zealand claimed (on rather slight evidence) that high interest rates in London had reduced their export receipts by depressing commodity prices; New Zealand further stated that this involved balance of payments difficulties and an outflow of short-term capital, which in turn had necessitated borrowing in London on very unfavourable terms. Even more emphatic was the comment from South Africa and Rhodesia, each with an economic structure responsive to capital movements: both reported that high interest rates in the United Kingdom during the years 1956–58 had adversely affected the balance of payments either through an outflow of capital or a check to the inflow: in the Union these trends were so marked that exchange controls had to be imposed on transactions with the sterling area.

As an alternative to the use of monetary policy for defensive purposes the Committee considered devaluation and reviewed the conditions in which it might be justified. Recognising that this was a matter which concerned other sterling countries and would raise complex policy issues, the conclusion was that the maintenance of a fixed rate of exchange minimised strains within the sterling area except in abnormal conditions when the world economy was out of balance and the system as a whole under pressure in relation to the non-sterling world.

The Committee did not study the effects of the post-war devaluation of sterling or consider whether it had been justified in the light of later history. Such a study might perhaps have proved of some utility since at any rate the circumstances exemplify the nature of the issues. Certain aspects of the crisis which bear on sterling area relationships may be recalled.

In 1949 the Commonwealth members of the system were informed by the United Kingdom of the imminent devaluation the day before it became effective. The new rate was applicable only to the currency of the United Kingdom and the Colonies: other members had then to decide whether to maintain the existing rate with sterling and thus depreciate as against the dollar, or maintain the existing rate with the dollar and thus appreciate as against sterling, or adopt an intermediate course. In fact the choice was governed mainly by the extent to which external receipts and payments were in sterling. The Indian Government, in explaining why it was necessary to devalue, put the case as follows:

> The sterling area is important to us in our international economic relations. A great part of our international trade is with this area; most of our export markets are also in this area and it is important that we should not only maintain but improve our export position. If we had not taken parallel action in revising the dollar-rupee ratio, the prices of our goods in our principal export countries would have risen immediately and that would have affected our trade interests and all those engaged in the work of production in our country. The devaluation of the pound therefore made the revision of the dollar-rupee rate almost unavoidable in the interests of our own country.

This statement indicates that the dollar balance of payments was only of secondary importance in determining exchange rate policy. Although devaluation increased the cost of dollar imports, these in most cases were relatively small, and there was also an opportunity to increase dollar earnings. Moreover, in countries where gold production played some part in the economy, devaluation increased the sterling price of the output: this factor was of course paramount in South Africa.

In the event all sterling countries except Pakistan decided to devalue. But the crisis even after ten years was recalled in the memoranda submitted by central banks to the Radcliffe Committee. Thus India pointed out that a pound of stable value was indispensable for the working of the sterling system and noted that the 1949 devaluation marked down the value of India's sterling balances in dollar terms; Ceylon expressed the view that such unilateral action by the United Kingdom was to be deprecated as tending to impair confidence in the availability of sterling for international use. Rhodesia also emphasised that the maintenance of the exchange value of sterling was a matter of concern to the Federation and welcomed assurances by the United Kingdom that no alteration was contemplated.

The full implications of policy measures such as devaluation or Bank Rate cannot here be traced but it is evident that the use of these instruments by the United Kingdom may produce marked reactions in the overseas sterling area. Reactions of this kind are merely concrete examples of the difficulties inherent in the essentially complex structure of the sterling system. In post-war years the working of the mechanism has raised a number of controversial issues and some must now be examined.

(vi) *The Debate on Sterling*

Criticism of the sterling system has since the war come from various sources. During the earlier post-war years the benefits of membership were not infrequently questioned in overseas sterling countries: it was implied that the balance of advantage lay chiefly with the United Kingdom and that for other countries membership was of doubtful value. More recently, certain critics in the United Kingdom itself have pointed out that the operation of the system imposes a burden on the centre and have urged that London should withdraw from some of its functions as banker and investor.

The debate has covered several specific topics, including the incidence of trade restrictions and the operation of the dollar pool, the utilisation of the sterling balances, and the problem of capital supply. The content of the criticism in each case may be briefly summarised.[1]

In the trade field it was sometimes suggested that the system favoured the United Kingdom by restricting access to other sources of supply. For some years after the war there were complaints that sterling countries were unable to obtain United Kingdom goods (especially capital goods) in adequate quantity while restrictions on dollar trade made it impracticable to remedy the shortage by importing from the United States; later, when exports came more freely, it was said that prices were not competitive with those for similar products from dollar sources. The pooling arrangements also gave rise to criticism: there were difficulties over the amounts of hard currency allocated to dollar

---

[1] A good deal of the criticism will be found in the symposium with contributions from economists in overseas sterling countries published in the *Bulletin of the O.U. Institute of Statistics*, November 1959.

deficit countries while those with a dollar surplus considered that it was utilised for the benefit of the United Kingdom.

Only a detailed survey would show whether such views had substance. No doubt the restrictions were irksome, especially in the earlier post-war years when supplies were scarce, but there has perhaps been a tendency to over-state the extent to which dollar goods were rationed: in the colonial territories, for example, even after the measures necessitated by the 1949 crisis, imports from the United States in 1950 constituted a higher proportion of total imports than before the war. Moreover, the gain to the overseas sterling area through the limitation of dollar supplies was seldom taken into account. Several examples could be quoted: the fact that United Kingdom restrictions on dollar foodstuffs favoured imports from sterling sources; the rapid expansion of the Rhodesian tobacco industry as a response to dollar-saving measures; and the opportunity for Ceylon and Malaya to export copra to India, although the Philippine product was cheaper. The view that United Kingdom exports were not competitively priced seems inconsistent with the fact that they secured an expanding market in the United States despite attempts to exclude them while it is also significant that when restrictions were lifted there was no upsurge of imports from dollar sources.[1]

Criticism of the dollar pool is another matter which needs scrutiny. Drawings from the pool are hardly an adequate measure of the facilities afforded to members of the overseas sterling area for the purchase of non-sterling goods since the E.P.U. mechanism enabled them to trade with Europe: moreover, in this context it would be proper to take into account the dollar content of a wide range of manufactures supplied by the United Kingdom. Critics of the system did not always put forward practicable alternatives: in particular, proposals to align the economy of an individual sterling country more closely with that of the United States were sometimes founded on dubious assumptions regarding the value of the United Kingdom market

---

[1] Between 1954 and 1959 the United States share of R.S.A. imports rose only from 12·3 per cent to 13·7 per cent (*Bulletin of National Institute for Economic and Social Research*, May 1960).

or the possibility of switching exports in order to earn a dollar surplus.

However confused the issues in the earlier post-war years it is clear that the sterling system is no longer based on controls discriminating against non-sterling trade. In 1950 imports into the overseas sterling area came in nearly equal proportions from the United Kingdom and non-sterling countries: for several years past, however, imports from non-sterling countries have exceeded £2,000 million per annum while imports from the United Kingdom have been of the order of £1,500 million. It should also be noted that during the past ten years United Kingdom exports to non-sterling countries have doubled (despite 'non-competitive' prices) while there has been only a 50 per cent increase in exports to the overseas sterling area: as a result non-sterling markets have become more important for the United Kingdom than markets in the sterling area. This trend has enabled the United Kingdom to attain near-equilibrium in its account with the non-sterling world while the overseas sterling area has been heavily in deficit.

Another major problem centred on the treatment of the post-war sterling balances. At first there was the possibility that some of them would be scaled down (as contemplated in the Anglo-American Loan Agreement) and even when this proposal was dropped certain sterling countries found part of their balances blocked and specific limitations placed on convertibility. Such formal restrictions were not in fact of much practical importance and within a few years the end-war balances were run down to levels which in several cases proved minimal. It cannot be said, therefore, that these assets were not utilised. Nor is there a much better case for the complaint that the real value of the remaining balances has been eroded through rising prices: this can hardly be regarded as peculiar to sterling since neither gold nor the dollar is proof against loss of purchasing power.

The colonial sterling balances in particular were a target for criticism. Here the post-war increase was commonly interpreted as representing investment by the Colonies in the United Kingdom and it was maintained that these funds would have been better employed if utilised for development purposes in the

Colonies. Such an interpretation is not consistent with the facts. The United Kingdom could borrow only if there was a surplus to lend but (as noted on p. 11) there is no evidence that the Colonies were able to earn a surplus: for the post-war period as a whole, therefore, they were not in a position to lend abroad and the increase in their balances must be attributed to capital receipts.

The fact that the Colonies are known to have been heavily dependent on such receipts leads to the general problem of capital supply. It has often been assumed that after the war the United Kingdom was no longer able to perform its traditional function of providing the resources needed for development in the overseas sterling area and it was therefore concluded that a developing country would have to look elsewhere for capital, re-orienting its economy accordingly.

This view is negatived by the figures available on post-war international investment. Capital exports from the United Kingdom have been very large and for the most part have been directed towards overseas sterling countries. On the other hand, it has not, in general, proved possible for these countries to satisfy any considerable part of their capital needs either in the United States or in Europe.

Alternatively it is sometimes stated that the United Kingdom has not been in a position to invest abroad to any great extent from its own resources and that recorded capital exports represent merely a transfer in that imported capital was passed on to other countries. These assertions are based on data drawn from the balance of payments estimates but closer scrutiny will show that neither is well-founded.

The validity of the first statement depends on the amount of the current surplus: the suggestion that this has been insufficient to allow scope for overseas investment can be refuted by showing that the inadequate treatment of reinvestment in the estimates vitiates the results: the evidence (referred to on p. 17) implies that a full statement would indicate an adequate surplus. It can also be shown that United Kingdom investment overseas was not merely the re-export of imported capital: the case here rests mainly on the assumption that such investment

was effected by borrowing from the Colonies but must be abandoned when it is shown that the Colonies had no surplus to lend.
Furthermore, it is disproved by the evidence that in recent years
the United Kingdom, which after the war was a net debtor on
international investment account, has regained creditor status.

It is clear that much of the criticism concerning capital
supplies as well as the sterling balances and trade restrictions
cannot be sustained. This conclusion involves the revision of
some accepted notions on policy issues.

In fact after ten years of criticism along the lines set out above,
a new turn was given to the discussion. The events of 1957
(when there was pressure on the reserves although the United
Kingdom had a comfortable surplus on its current balance)
provided the occasion for a reconsideration of recent history.
The circumstances suggested that the reserve crises encountered
by the United Kingdom in post-war years could be attributed
to its responsibilities as the focal point of the sterling area. To
obviate such difficulties, the advocates of this view supported
measures which ranged from the dismantling of the system to
specific proposals for eliminating excess sterling balances or
curtailing overseas investment.[1]

An official statement of United Kingdom policy intended to
rebut the arguments of those who wished to liquidate the sterling
system is reproduced on pp. 117–119. The Treasury put a
somewhat similar case before the Radcliffe Committee.[2]

In evidence the Treasury told the Committee that it was not
possible to wind up the sterling area, if only because the United
Kingdom's international liabilities far exceeded its assets. There
seem to be no grounds for this assertion. More firmly based was
the suggestion that liquidation by the United Kingdom might
adversely affect confidence, and in any case the system was
deemed to be a link in the totality of Commonwealth relationships. From the technical aspect sterling was considered to be
indispensable because it could be utilised for international trade
over a wide area and could not be replaced by any other system

---

[1] A summary account will be found in the P.E.P. pamphlet *The Debate on Sterling*
(Planning, No. 421, April 1958).
[2] Minutes of Evidence, Q. 2531.

c

or currency: in particular, the centralisation of operations in London represented an economy in reserves and thus permitted a more liberal trading policy than would otherwise be practicable. The general bias of the Treasury case was thus against change.

A similar attitude is apparent in the overseas sterling area, at least in official circles, where there does not seem to have been any marked reaction to the new policy debate. Little trace of its influence can be found in the memoranda submitted to the Radcliffe Committee by the central banks of sterling countries: although comment was invited on the functioning of the system, the invitation elicited few recommendations for change. The memoranda include critical remarks on specific points but no evidence of general dissatisfaction or of any intention to terminate the existing arrangements. Thus the Commonwealth Bank of Australia noted that the sterling area was based on considerations of mutual interest and provided a framework within which trade could develop with relative freedom: the dollar pool, in particular, enabled Australia to finance its trade with the dollar area smoothly and efficiently. The New Zealand Reserve Bank said that an attempt had not been made to weigh up the pros and cons of the system but no alternative had ever been seriously considered. The Central Bank of Ceylon (a dollar surplus country) expressed the view that it was to Ceylon's advantage to remain within the area as external trade was financed in sterling and international reserves held in sterling. The Reserve Bank of India considered that the convertibility of sterling was the main advantage to member countries. In general it will be found that while the earlier criticism was reflected only to a limited extent in the memoranda, the more radical recent proposals were hardly mentioned.

A decision to maintain the system in essentials would not necessarily preclude the adoption of certain changes. One proposal, an attempt to eliminate excess sterling balances, recalls the discussions at the end of the war and the terms of the Anglo-American Loan Agreement. It was now revived by those who held that the size of the balances constituted an element of instability in the sterling mechanism.

The suggestion receives support from the Treasury's emphasis on the need for a better balance between reserves and liabilities. Even with an adequate presentation of the ratio it might be advisable to effect some improvement and this could be done in different ways. The Radcliffe Committee noted that the Treasury expressed no decided preference as between increasing reserves or reducing liabilities: the Committee itself discussed possible methods of dealing with the reserves but did not consider in detail whether a reduction in the sterling balances was practicable. The point may be examined here.

An assessment of the position as at the end of 1956 is given in the Bank of England paper on the sterling balances (pp. 62–67). It was then judged that the holdings of non-sterling countries had in general been reduced to 'a natural (perhaps low) working level'. Much the same was true of the independent Commonwealth countries: the Bank considered that none except India held sterling well above a reasonable minimum (since then India's balances have been heavily reduced). This left only two groups with holdings which could be regarded as unreasonably large: the Middle East oil countries and the colonial territories (including those which have lately become independent).

It can perhaps be said that the figures for the oil countries are not of overwhelming magnitude: at the end of 1956 they represented rather less than one-tenth of the total. On the other hand there has been since the war an enormous increase in the balances of the colonial territories, which have latterly accounted for over one-third of the total. Such a large accumulation of sterling does not necessarily denote the existence of surplus balances in any real sense but is an attribute of the colonial economy: these funds, which arise out of transactions connected with currency, banking and public finance, are held in London primarily because of limited investment facilities in the territories overseas.

The assessment indicates that there is little scope for proposals designed to effect a reduction in the balances. This conclusion is supported by post-war history. For the independent Commonwealth countries the record shows that it has rarely been possible to maintain a satisfactory margin over minimum needs. At one time or another Australia, New Zealand, South Africa and India (to name only the most notable cases) have drawn down their holdings to a point where emergency measures were needed to prevent further depletion: the same could be said of other countries in the group. Such difficulties have long been regarded as a function of the instability which characterises the balance of payments in a primary producing country: experience shows that if they are to be avoided, it is necessary to hold relatively large external assets.

Any attempt to deal with the problem must take account of these facts. Although the scaling-down of excess balances as contemplated in the Anglo-American Financial Agreement of 1945 is no longer a practical possibility, other plans have been put forward from time to time. It has, for example, been proposed that the position should be corrected by selling overseas investments to nationals of the countries concerned. There is perhaps something to be said for reducing the Middle East holdings in this way: the offer of a half-share in the oil companies might well be preferable to having the investment nationalised at some future date. The general effect would not, however, be very great as the Middle East balances constitute quite a small proportion of the total. In other cases the plan could be adopted only where individual countries were able to spare funds for the purpose: it does not seem likely to have widespread application or significant results. Similarly, the suggestion that the colonial balances should be repaid is impracticable unless there are radical changes in the organisation of colonial currency, banking and finance: such changes would involve the abolition of sterling cover for note issues as well as restrictions on the use of the London money market.

The evidence implies that the existing sterling balances do not, for the most part, admit of a planned reduction. The Radcliffe Committee itself came to this conclusion, pointing out that a rapid reduction in the total would be inadvisable as it would tend to reduce the liquidity of overseas monetary systems: 'We should refrain from seizing too eagerly on the opportunity of extinguishing short-term debts as a means of strengthening . . .

the pound sterling. . . . We should ourselves be inclined to lay more emphasis on the need to increase the reserves than on the desirability of an absolute reduction in liabilities.'

The other major proposal put forward by those who thought that the operation of the sterling system imposed too great a burden on the United Kingdom concerned the export of capital: it was held that this adversely affected the level of domestic investment and involved some strain on the balance of payments. Expressed in such terms the proposition was neither novel nor radical: for a number of years a measure of control had been operated as a means of reducing pressure on the reserves. The suggestion that control should be intensified was, however, of special importance because of its impact on several members of the overseas sterling area.

Estimates published in the Report of the Committee show that existing restrictions had not reduced overseas investment to negligible proportions. In fact post-war performance in this field compares not unfavourably with the pre-war record: the figures indicate a rate of capital export which even in real terms may well have been greater than that attained at the end of the 19th century, when conditions both in the United Kingdom and abroad were in many respects more favourable.

It could be maintained that in the changed conditions of to-day capital exports on such a scale were no longer justifiable, especially as they worked against a reduction in the sterling balances. On the other hand, all the memoranda from overseas sterling countries refer to their dependence on the United Kingdom for capital supplies and some in terms which attest the importance of this factor. India and Ceylon both stated that development capital had not been received in adequate quantity (without reference to the possibility that official policy in those countries might have been partly responsible): Australia and Rhodesia acknowledged that the United Kingdom had provided a large amount of capital, although in each case the restrictions on issues in the London market were criticised. South Africa (which since the war has received more capital from the United Kingdom than any other country) also mentioned obstacles to the free flow of funds, stating that the Union considered this flow of great importance and regarded it as an essential feature of the sterling system.

The Radcliffe Committee pronounced against any attempt to increase reserves by further restrictions on overseas investment. For this decision the Committee gave three reasons: the need to encourage Commonwealth development; the fact that overseas investment helped United Kingdom trade and was expected by members of the overseas sterling area; and the probability that the gain to the reserves would be unlikely to equal the fall in capital exports. The substance of the argument is reproduced on pp. 97–99.

Examination of policy issues such as capital flows or the sterling balances no less than policy measures such as devaluation or Bank Rate brings out in concrete detail the complexity of the inter-relationships which subsist within the sterling system: these clearly extend over a wide range of economic activity from merchandise trade to banking and finance. The process of policy-making has to be carried on in this context, with due regard to the claims of each sector. It has also to take account of the interests, not always identical, of the different members of the system in an attempt to reach decisions which will represent a fair balance of advantage.

The Radcliffe Committee came to the conclusion that the general harmony of interests between the United Kingdom and other sterling countries was the vital element in the problem (pp. 119–122). Such an approach does not, however, absolve from the duty of analysing specific technical issues. A study of the documents presented in this book should make it clear that if policy is to be firmly based, the facts on such issues should be plainly set out in order that the problem can be assessed in all its bearings.

TEXTS

I

THE STERLING AREA

(Memorandum submitted by H.M. Treasury to the Radcliffe Committee. Source: *Principal Memoranda of Evidence*, Vol. I)

A. Introductory

1. The object of this paper is to describe the Sterling Area. It is a factual paper. Clearly there arise from it problems of the first importance for domestic monetary policy. These problems are discussed in the separate paper being submitted by the Treasury entitled 'Monetary Policy and External Economic Problems'.

2. Section B discusses briefly the origins and present operation of the Area. Section C deals with its recent history in terms of its impact on the United Kingdom's external reserves and liabilities.

B. The Sterling Area and System

3. 'The Sterling Area' is far from being a term with a precise meaning. Treated as a list of countries there is no ambiguity: it consists of the 'Scheduled Territories' (including the United Kingdom) as defined in the United Kingdom's Exchange Control Act 1947 (in which the words 'Sterling Area' do not, incidentally, occur). But the term is more usually and more usefully regarded as more than a geographical grouping. It is essentially a group of countries, most but not all of them members of the Commonwealth, who follow generally comparable policies in their overseas financial transactions.

4. The sterling system originated in the first half of the nineteenth century in the process of bringing some order into the heterogeneous coinage systems and rudimentary banking arrangements which then prevailed in most of the Colonies. The system which grew from these origins had four characteristics:

First, the local currencies and bank-notes were statutorily regulated as local versions of the pound, printed or stamped with local symbols but all representing the sovereign or legally defined fractions of it, and all backed with some obligatory holding of sovereigns or gold.

Secondly, all looked to London as their metropolitan centre for the employment of surplus funds which could not be invested with the necessary liquidity in the colonial countries themselves.

Thirdly, as trade increased, all looked to sterling as the currency for their external transactions. There were some local exceptions to this: for example, the Indian rupee had, and still has, an international validity in the countries round the Indian Ocean, but with all other areas India settles in sterling.

Fourthly, all looked to London and the United Kingdom for the raising of new capital, predominantly for private enterprise but largely also for governmental, provincial or municipal issues.

It must be noted too that, besides these monetary links with London, London was and has remained the centre for such connected commercial activities as merchanting, insurance, shipping, etc.

5. In such a system the gravitation of the foreign exchange income of the whole area to London was a natural and inevitable consequence of normal business and banking practices. Exporters sold their export proceeds to their local banks against the local currency in which they kept their accounts and met their expenses. Most often the proceeds so sold were already in the form of sterling and any foreign exchange arising had already accrued directly or indirectly to London; when another currency was involved, ordinary practice led the bankers to convert it into sterling as their common external currency or common source of liquidity for surplus funds, and the same result followed; the foreign exchange gravitated to London. Exchange control played no part in this natural centralisation of foreign exchange income and surpluses at the metropolitan centre.

6. Despite the great changes of the last thirty or forty years and the establishment of exchange controls throughout the area during the last war and their subsequent persistence, these four pre-1914 characteristics still largely hold for the sterling area

today. But there have been developments inside and outside the area which have to some extent modified the characteristics of the system:

(a) The free interchangeability between sterling and gold, which established a guarantee of the value and a limitation on the volume of sterling, has been removed. The first step was taken in 1931 when the United Kingdom abandoned the gold standard. A wide group of countries, including all Commonwealth countries except Canada, immediately or soon after pegged their own currencies on sterling, though some continued to maintain substantial reserves of their own in gold and all were entirely free to acquire it against sterling. In 1939 they agreed not to make use of this facility, except for essential current payments.

(b) In 1939, exchange controls were introduced generally in the United Kingdom and other sterling area countries, but they were not applied to transactions between the United Kingdom and the R.S.A. (rest of the sterling area).

(c) Most of the independent members of the area now have central banks of their own and most are members of the International Monetary Fund with par values for their currencies defined in terms of gold or the United States dollar. In most of them legislation between the wars provided for sterling having a mandatory place in the currency backing. In many cases post-war enactments have removed such provisions, and the sterling backing is now discretionary rather than mandatory. Thus the currency link is no longer a statutory obligation. But despite this, in practice it has been maintained: all R.S.A. countries devalued to the same extent as the United Kingdom in 1949, with the sole exception of Pakistan who, however, followed six years later and restored her old relationship with the £; moreover the R.S.A. countries have also in practice maintained a fixed link in day-to-day fluctuations of the £.

(d) During the 1939–45 War, a huge accumulation of sterling

balances took place. (The main growth in colonial sterling balances and the holdings of the Middle East Oil States came later and was substantially offset by falls in other countries' balances.) Moreover, as a result of the growth of exchange controls, these balances came, to a greater extent than before, to be held in the control of central banks and to be treated as national foreign exchange reserves, their size and trend becoming objects of national policy just as are those of our own gold and dollar reserves.

(e) The widespread use in the area of discriminatory trade restrictions against dollar, and sometimes against all nonsterling, imports has been a significant feature in the war and post-war years. This policy has of course been pursued with very varying degrees of strictness by the different members of the area, and in the last few years discrimination has been greatly reduced. This whole evolution has been closely affected by the desire of the area's members to preserve both the status of sterling as an international currency and the security of their sterling holdings. Hence some measure of discrimination has been for some years (though to a steadily diminishing extent) one of the practices, *de facto*, of the area.

(f) London has remained the prime source of new capital for the R.S.A. and a very large outflow has been maintained since the war. This traditional position has been so far maintained despite the emergence of the International Bank for Reconstruction and Development as an increasingly large lender, of United States aid in grants and loans and of increasing United States private investment. The outflow to the R.S.A. is now distinguished from United Kingdom investment in Canada and other nonsterling countries by being free from the requirement of exchange control approval.

(g) Conversely, strict control of investment in the nonsterling world by residents of the sterling area was imposed by individual exchange controls in all parts of the area during the war and has been maintained (though in varying degrees and with some relaxations) ever since. This broad objective of exchange control has therefore come also to be thought of as another of the sterling area's normal practices.

7. Thus the sterling area in recent years has been in many respects a continuation of the traditional set of arrangements of the pre-war sterling system. The underlying characteristics of the area remain little changed. They have been overlaid by changed circumstances and new pressures on sterling arising in the post-war situation, which have presented special problems; and the mechanisms of controls evolved to meet these problems may at times have appeared to be essential features of the sterling system. These have varied from time to time and from member to member. For example, for the Persian Gulf State members of the sterling area, exchange control is of a very limited character. But in fact the fundamental features of membership of the sterling area remain:

(a) The members use sterling as the normal means of external settlement;

(b) They hold the major part of their reserves in sterling;

(c) They look to the United Kingdom as a major source of external capital;

(d) They co-operate to maintain the strength of sterling.

8. World trade depends upon an adequate payments mechanism. It is vital to the United Kingdom that such a mechanism should be maintained, both because of our national interest in world economic progress and because of our dependence on international trade. Sterling plays the major role in this, and there is no substitute for it. Certain particular advantages flow from this position of sterling. First, United Kingdom citizens, because they are able to use their own currency over a large part of the world, are themselves saved the inconveniences of operating in foreign currencies, and they have access to vital raw materials on the most favourable terms on the commodity markets established in the United Kingdom. Second, sterling as an international currency brings similar advantages to the other members of the sterling area and to the Commonwealth as a whole. Finally, the banking, insurance and similar transac-

tions carried out in London based upon the international character of sterling are in themselves profitable.

9. But the counterpart of these advantages is the greater risks to which we are exposed from the considerable sterling balances which other countries hold. Whenever doubt is cast on our solvency these balances come under pressure, thus tending to aggravate the very situation that caused the doubts to arise. The use of sterling as an international currency makes it inevitable that we should have large overseas monetary liabilities. But it does not explain their present size, which derives from economic developments in the war and post-war years and has little to do with the normal requirements of a centre for international finance. The international strength of sterling would obviously be greater if the balances could be reduced without any corresponding reduction in the reserves. Meanwhile that sterling is an international currency and that the countries of the sterling area hold large quantities are facts of the situation which have to be reckoned with in all our economic policies.

10. The cohesion and viability of the sterling area depend above all on the strength of sterling. The factors determining this are of the greatest complexity, but they express themselves ultimately in changes in the relationship between our gold and dollar reserves and overseas sterling holdings.[1] It will therefore be useful next to analyse in some detail the forces which operate upon our reserves and liabilities. This is done in the next section.

C. Reserves and Liabilities

11. Underlying the movements in our reserves and liabilities there is a pattern of flows of funds for commercial and financial reasons. Among these there is a useful distinction between those

---

[1] 'The reserves' comprise gold and holdings of convertible foreign currencies in the Exchange Equalisation Account. At the time when this paper was submitted the only such currencies held by the E.E.A. were United States and Canadian dollars; hence the reserves were often (as in this paper) described as 'the gold and dollar reserves'. Since December 1958 a number of other foreign currencies have become convertible, and E.E.A. holdings of these currencies fall to be included in 'the reserves', in the sense in which they are discussed in this paper. 'Overseas sterling holdings' in this paper are as defined in *United Kingdom Balance of Payments 1946 to 1956* (No. 2) (Cmnd. 122), p. 54.

arising out of the United Kingdom's own balance of payments with the rest of the world, and those which derive from the impact on the United Kingdom's position of the use of sterling by the outside world.

12. In a country which is neither an international banker nor an international investor or borrower, a current account surplus on its external balance of payments will be reflected in an increase of the reserves; and the contrary for a deficit. But this simple effect is greatly modified for the United Kingdom by its large and complex external monetary relationships. These additional complications are of three sorts: (i) those introduced by the normal practice of the R.S.A. with respect to its non-sterling earnings; (ii) those introduced by long-term investment flows; and (iii) those introduced by the existence of large sterling holdings in N.S.A. (non-sterling area) countries. The effects of these may be considered as successive modifications to an initial simple state of affairs:

(a) The United Kingdom Current Balance

The normal position of the United Kingdom current balance is to be in surplus, a large surplus with the R.S.A. more than counterbalancing a deficit with the N.S.A. Ignoring all three of the complications just mentioned—i.e. assuming there are no long-term capital flows, that we deal with the R.S.A. only in sterling and their non-sterling trade has no impact on us, and the N.S.A. holds only gold, dollars and other non-sterling currencies—this would lead us to expect that normally or 'naturally' our sterling liabilities to the R.S.A. would be falling (as a result of the settlement of our R.S.A. surplus) and our reserves would also be falling, though less fast (as we settle the smaller N.S.A. deficit). Our net monetary position would be improving by the extent of our overall surplus, but this improvement would take the form of a reduction of liabilities larger than a simultaneous reduction in assets.

(b) The R.S.A. Current Balance

However the first complication is that the net proceeds of the R.S.A.'s trade with the N.S.A. normally gravitate to London and, just as it is normally in deficit with us (the obverse of our surplus with it), it is normally in surplus with the N.S.A. (including gold sales). Thus the sterling we pay to the R.S.A. in exchange for this R.S.A. surplus with the N.S.A. counteracts the fall in R.S.A. sterling holdings induced by our surplus with the R.S.A., while simultaneously the non-sterling currencies we receive counteract the loss of reserves we suffer from our deficit with the N.S.A. How this finally works out in terms of R.S.A. sterling holdings and United Kingdom reserves will depend upon whether the R.S.A. is in overall surplus or deficit, i.e. on whether its N.S.A. surplus exceeds or falls short of its deficit with the United Kingdom. The two cases can be illustrated schematically, assuming in both cases a United Kingdom overall surplus on the 'normal' pattern:

Case I

United Kingdom in overall surplus: R.S.A.
in overall surplus

	(1) U.K. current balance with	(2) R.S.A. current balance with	(1 and 2) Total Sterling Area current balance with
N.S.A.	—100	+300	+200
R.S.A.	+200		
U.K.		—200	
Total	+100	+100	+200

In this case the United Kingdom loses 100 of reserves to the N.S.A. in its own trade, but gains 300 (against payment of sterling to the R.S.A.) from R.S.A. trade with the N.S.A.: i.e. the reserves rise 200. But the payment of 300 of sterling against the R.S.A.'s N.S.A. transfers exceeds the receipt of 200 from the R.S.A. in respect of its deficit with us. Hence the 100 improvement in our balance of liabilities against assets consists of a gain of 200 to the reserves and an increase of 100 in our liabilities to the R.S.A., which latter is of course the R.S.A.'s increase in its external reserves due to its overall surplus.

CASE II

United Kingdom in overall surplus: R.S.A.
in overall deficit

	(1) U.K. current balance with	(2) R.S.A. current balance with	(1 and 2) Total Sterling Area current balance with
N.S.A.	—100	+50	—50
R.S.A.	+200		
U.K.		—200	
Total	+100	—150	—50

Here the United Kingdom's loss of 100 of reserves to the N.S.A. is not fully offset by its purchase of 50 from the R.S.A., so the reserves fall 50. But equally the 50 of sterling paid to the R.S.A. does not fully offset the 200 received in respect of our current balance so that our liabilities to the R.S.A. fall 150. The improvement in our position is still 100, our current surplus, but it takes a different form from that in Case I. In fact the R.S.A.'s current balance determines the form in which but not the amount by which our net monetary position improves.

It will be noted in both tables that the change in the reserves (on the assumptions so far made) is equal to the total sterling area balance with the N.S.A., and that this is calculable either as the sum of the United Kingdom's and R.S.A.'s non-sterling balance of payments or as the sum of their overall balance of payments (mutual balances of course cancelling out). From the United Kingdom point of view in particular it is of course vital to know whether, when the reserves are increasing, this is arising from a R.S.A. or a United Kingdom overall surplus; for in the first case the increase is matched by a rise in sterling liabilities to the R.S.A., and in the latter case it is not.

(c) Overseas Long-term Investment

The United Kingdom is habitually a large investor overseas, and the greater part of the investment is in the R.S.A. To the

D

extent that the United Kingdom invests in this way its current account surplus with the R.S.A. does not result in a reduction in the R.S.A.'s sterling holdings, and our investment in the N.S.A. equally reduces the receipt or increases the outflow of reserves arising from current trade. In respect of its effect upon reserves and liabilities, payment for a long-term capital asset is exactly the same as payment for a current asset. Thus when analysing changes in reserves and liabilities the balance of current and long-term capital transactions taken together is the relevant concept; not the current balance alone.

(d) N.S.A. Sterling Holdings

The final complication arises because N.S.A. countries may not in fact settle any deficit with the sterling area in gold or dollars or take gold or dollars in settlement of a surplus with the sterling area. Because they hold large quantities of sterling they can settle deficits with this, and, if they are so willing they can accept an increase in their sterling holdings in settlement of a surplus. Thus the final result of a sterling area surplus with the N.S.A. may be a running down of N.S.A. sterling holdings, without gain to the reserves, and equally a sterling area deficit may increase sterling liabilities to the N.S.A. rather than reduce reserves. In both cases the sterling area's net position vis-a-vis the N.S.A. will be changed by the amount of the surplus or deficit, but the form in which the change expresses itself, in reserves or in liabilities, will depend on the choice of N.S.A. countries. The choice made will of course depend largely on the state of confidence. It is perfectly possible, if confidence is bad, for a sterling area surplus with the N.S.A. to be accompanied by a fall in reserves and a still larger fall in N.S.A. sterling holdings. But the most dangerous situation is obviously one in which both the United Kingdom and the R.S.A. are in deficit on current and long-term capital account, for then both the joint sterling area deficit and a reduction of N.S.A. sterling holdings for confidence reasons may combine to have a drastic impact on the reserves.

13. Thus, some of the factors affecting the strength of sterling may be regarded as 'internal', as arising primarily from policies and decisions within the United Kingdom, namely:

(*a*) the United Kingdom balance of payments on current account, and

(*b*) United Kingdom overseas investment;

whilst other factors are 'external', as arising primarily from policies and decisions elsewhere, namely:

(*c*) the current balance of payments of the R.S.A., and

(*d*) the amount of sterling which the N.S.A. chooses to hold.

This distinction between 'internal' and 'external' influences is convenient. It must, however, be remembered that the United Kingdom's current surplus with the R.S.A. is the same thing as the R.S.A.'s current deficit with the United Kingdom; that many unpredictable events originating outside the United Kingdom affect the out-turn of the United Kingdom's balance of payments, however wise our internal policies; and that action (or inaction) in this country will greatly influence decisions which are formally 'external'. It is, however, useful to make this separation in order to observe that the 'internal' factors affect the size of gap between the reserves and the liabilities, but the 'external' do not, the current balance of payments of the R.S.A. determining whether a United Kingdom surplus narrows the gap by increasing the reserves or by decreasing the R.S.A. sterling balances (or by a bit of both), and the N.S.A. holding of sterling affecting both reserves and liabilities equally.

14. The picture which emerges is that, in present circumstances, a current account surplus in the United Kingdom balance of payments is of fundamental importance to the whole strength and soundness of sterling, though it does not in itself ensure either a reduction of the sterling balances or an increase in the reserves. Overseas investment (which is natural and beneficial to us and the recipients and with which the normal current account surplus is largely bound up) works against a reduction of the sterling balances; and the withdrawal of sterling balances held by the N.S.A. will, so long as it continues, work against an increase in the reserves—all this in spite of a substantial United Kingdom current surplus in most years. In short, it is only when we have a surplus on current account greater than our net

investment overseas that we are able to improve our external monetary position (whether by reducing the total of the sterling balances or by increasing the reserves).

15. *Recent Experience.* This analysis can be illustrated from the figures published in Balance of Payments White Papers. (In the statistics which follow, estimates of long-term capital movements (which are subject to a considerable margin of error) are shown only to the nearest £10 million and other totals are here rounded to the nearest £5 million.)

16. During 1953–56 the pattern of the United Kingdom's total balance of payments on current and long-term capital account was as follows:

		£ Million	
United Kingdom	*R.S.A.*	*N.S.A.*	*Total*
Identified current account	+960	—375	+585
Identified long-term capital (net outflow)	—680	—155	—835
Total	+280	—530	—250
Unidentified receipts			+100
Total			—150

Thus, during 1953–56 the United Kingdom had a total current account surplus of £585 million. But in the same period there were long-term investment and loan repayments of £835 million. The difference between these two figures, both resulting from what have been called 'internal causes', was £250 million. This was reduced by about £100 million of net unidentified receipts by the United Kingdom (the balancing item). Nevertheless £150 million was left, as the measure of the net increase in what might be called our short-term or monetary liabilities over the four years.

17. During the same period, however, the balance of payments of the R.S.A. as a whole (its individual members had widely differing experiences) was as follows:

£ Million

R.S.A.	U.K.	N.S.A.	Total
Identified current account	—960	+ 765	—195
Identified long-term capital (net inflow)	+ 680	*	+ 680
Total	—280	+ 765	+ 485
Unidentified payments			—130
Total			+ 355

* Gold sales, Official Aid (grants and loans) and identified non-sterling capital transactions, both long and short-term, are here included in the 'current' account.

This produced two results:

(i) The fact that the surplus of £765 million with the N.S.A. and the receipts of capital of £680 million from the United Kingdom were together more than sufficient to offset the deficit of £960 million on current account with the United Kingdom and other net unidentified payments to the United Kingdom of £130 million, enabled the R.S.A. to add £355 million to its monetary assets in the United Kingdom.

(ii) But the £765 million of net non-sterling receipts was more than sufficient to pay for the United Kingdom's deficit with the N.S.A. of £530 million. When allowance was made for small unidentified payments by the United Kingdom to the N.S.A., £210 million was left over. This was available either to raise our reserves or reduce our N.S.A. liabilities and, broadly speaking, the choice was for the N.S.A. to make. It would have led to a rise in the reserves if the non-sterling world, taken together, had chosen to hold the same amount of sterling at the end of 1956 as at the beginning of 1953. It would have led to a fall in our N.S.A. liabilities had the whole net non-sterling earnings been absorbed in repaying liabilities. In fact, non-sterling countries drew down their net sterling assets by about £100 million and we paid off £95 million of our debt in E.P.U. But since the sterling holdings of non-territorial organisations rose £100 million (due to net purchases of dollars from the I.M.F.) our non-sterling assets rose by £115 million and our non-sterling liabilities fell by about £95 million.

18. Detailed figures of our monetary assets and liabilities as defined for balance of payments purposes are given below.

	£ Million		
	End *1952*	*End* *1956*	*Change* *1953–56*
Assets			
1. Gold and dollar reserves	659	799*	+ 140
2. Official holdings of non-dollar currencies	40	14	—26
3. Total (1 + 2)	699	813	+ 114
Liabilities			
4. R.S.A. sterling holdings	2,542	2,860	+ 318
5. N.S.A. countries' sterling holdings	677	565	—112
Total sterling holdings of countries	3,219	3,425	+ 206
6. Non-territorial organisations' sterling holdings	567	669	+ 102
7. U.K. debt to E.P.U.	219	125	—94
8. Total (4 + 5 + 6 + 7)	4,005	4,219	+ 214
9. Total net (8—3)	3,306	3,406	+ 100
10. Net change in other miscellaneous identified assets and liabilities			+ 50
11. Total net change in identified assets and liabilities (9 + 10)			+ 150

* Including £37 million of dollars paid into special accounts in December, 1956 and returned to the gold and dollar reserves in April, 1957.

19. This 'balance sheet' of the overseas monetary position does not describe our overall position precisely; the liabilities include an incalculable but large amount which is not really a liquid liability as normally understood. The dividing line between long and short is essentially arbitrary. Statistically it can only be defined in terms of the nature of the asset or liability, and not by the purpose or attitude of the holder (though this is the characteristic more relevant to policy); e.g. a Treasury Bill held in a legally fixed currency backing is technically a short-term liability, but unless the legislation is altered, it can reasonably be expected that the cash will be steadily reinvested in Treasury Bills. The liability can therefore, in another sense, be regarded as a long-term investment in the United Kingdom. Or again, a long-term United Kingdom Government security is a very liquid, easily realisable asset and may be purchased by a non-resident for some explicitly short-term purpose, but the formal classification of the purchase in our balance of payments figures does not necessarily reflect the intentions of the holder. In point of fact the return of overseas sterling holdings from which a major part of the figures given above is built up includes a good many long-term and short-term securities held for long-term purposes (the definition is given in the Balance of Payments White Papers). It therefore certainly exaggerates the scale of our genuinely short-term or monetary or liquid liabilities. On the other hand the assets are of a strictly cash kind. Hence, the *changes* in the balance between these assets and liabilities between successive years probably describe the total *change* in our liquid position much more accurately than the total figures describe the *absolute* position at any one time.

II

THE STERLING BALANCES

(Extracted from *New Contributions to Economic Statistics*, H.M.S.O., 1959)

I Introduction

1. In recent years figures of overseas sterling holdings have been published every half year in the United Kingdom Balance of Payments White Papers.

2. Section II deals with the series on overseas sterling holdings and acceptances, and Section III shortly discusses the relationship between these items, the gold and dollar reserves, and the overseas monetary position of the United Kingdom.

II Statistics of Overseas Sterling Holdings

3. The overseas sterling holdings series originated with the figures of banks' liabilities and assets on overseas account which were included in the Report of Committee on Finance and Industry (the 'Macmillan' Committee) in 1931 and which on their recommendation were regularly collected thereafter. Figures broadly comparable with the present series can be carried back to 1941, but during the war the scope of the compilation was progressively broadened in order to obtain a more comprehensive measure of the increase which then took place in the country's overseas liabilities. Accordingly, the end of 1945 is taken as the starting point of the series for the purpose of this paper; for earlier figures reference should be made to *Reserves and Liabilities 1931 to 45*, Cmd. 8354 of September 1951.

4. Each month the Bank of England receives reports on a voluntary basis from over 150 institutions, namely, all commercial banks in the United Kingdom with significant overseas

connections (including the United Kingdom offices of overseas banks as well as accepting and discount houses) and a number of official bodies such as the Crown Agents for Oversea Governments and Administrations, the various Currency Boards and the West African Marketing Boards.

5. Each reporting bank in the United Kingdom is asked to give three items for each overseas country:

(i) Its net liability to (or net asset with) its overseas offices. (It is not practicable to obtain gross figures of liabilities and assets vis-a-vis overseas branches because of differences in accounting procedure.)

(ii) The gross amount due from it on its own account and on account of its United Kingdom customers to other overseas residents (other banks, companies, individuals).

(iii) The gross amount due to it on its own account and on account of its United Kingdom customers from overseas residents other than its own offices.

Residence is determined by Exchange Control classification insofar as non-sterling area countries are concerned, and for sterling area accounts by registered address of a company or permanent domicile of any other account holder.

6. *Definition.* The funds at present reported comprise:[1]

(i) Holdings in sterling or sterling area currencies (whether as desposits, advances or commercial bills or Treasury Bills, or British Government securities if held for account of overseas banks) of account holders abroad with banks in the United Kingdom; net of claims of similar types by banks in the United Kingdom on overseas banks and other residents abroad; (i.e. the sum of the three subtotals referred to above).

(ii) Funds, now small, held for account of the United States Government, for their own use or for help to third countries, originating from the sterling equivalent of dollars made available under United States aid legislation.

(iii) Sterling funds held with the Crown Agents for Oversea

---

[1] The most useful composition is a matter for discussion, depending on the purpose of the statistics, and is therefore subject to review.

TABLE I
Sterling Holdings by area and Class of Holder

£ million

	End 1945			End 1951			End 1957		
	Total	Central bank and other official funds	Other funds	Total	Central bank and other official funds	Other funds	Total	Central bank and other official funds	Other funds
Sterling area countries									
United Kingdom Colonies	411	263	148	919	703	216	1,269	1,023	246
Other sterling area countries	1,986	1,702	284	1,717	1,590	127	1,430	1,184	246
Total sterling area countries	2,397	1,965	432	2,636	2,293	343	2,699	2,207	492
Non-sterling countries									
Dollar area	34	15	19	38	28	10	35	4	31
Other western hemisphere countries	163	158	5	57	39	18	31	13	18
O.E.E.C. countries	351	190	161	328	158	170	258	130	128
Other non-sterling countries	622	432	190	518	399	119	244	154	90
Total non-sterling countries	1,170	795	375	941	624	317	568	301	267
Total: all countries	3,567	2,760	807	3,577	2,917	660	3,267	2,508	759
Non-territorial organisations	—		—	566	566	—	645	645	—

Governments and Administrations and by Currency Boards, excluding Dominion and Colonial sterling securities.

(iv) So far as known, British Government securities held by other official bodies but not those held by private individuals or firms.

Throughout securities are taken at their nominal value.

7. *Analysis of holdings.* Various classifications of overseas sterling holdings are possible. The most important are those by area, by class of holder and by type of asset held. For the purposes of a short general account of the holdings it is convenient to take the first two together.

8. *Holdings by area and class of holder.* Table I shows total holdings at the end of 1945, 1951 and 1957 classified by area[1] and by the two principal types of holder, central bank and other official funds so far as separate figures are available on the one hand, and funds with commercial banks on the other. The latter may include funds held by overseas official bodies, but probably only to a small extent.

(i) *Colonial Holdings*

9. The main classes of Colonial funds at the end of 1945, 1951 and 1957 were as shown in Table II on p. 52.

Similar figures for recent half-years are published regularly with a territorial analysis of total funds in the *Digest of Colonial Statistics* where, however, Dominion and Colonial sterling securities are included.

10. The existence of currency and many other funds in sterling is largely explained by the fact that the Colonies do not yet possess developed local capital markets and hence hold in London the very large funds governments must hold for many and diverse purposes. Colonial currencies are very largely backed by sterling securities. The steadily increasing circulations which have accompanied rising populations, the increased use of money and increasing external incomes have thus produced a virtually automatic increase in the investment by Currency

[1] The geographical divisions used in this article and the tables incorporated in the text, are the same for all periods and in general correspond to those used in the Balance of Payments White Paper (Cmnd. 399).

TABLE II

Sterling Holdings of Colonial Territories: Distribution
by class of fund

	1945	1951	1957
	£ million at end of year		
Currency funds	148	312	441
Special funds with Crown Agents[1]	74	112	154
General funds with Crown Agents[2]	41	148	321
Miscellaneous official funds[3]	—	131	107
Other funds (with United Kingdom banks)	148	216	246
Total	411	919	1,269

[1] Funds of Colonial Governments and other public bodies held under statute or earmarked for special purposes (sinking funds, savings banks' funds, etc.).

[2] General revenue balances, general purpose reserve funds, etc.

[3] Uganda Price Assistance Funds, sterling securities of West African Marketing Boards, etc.

Boards in United Kingdom and other government securities. Special funds, the largest component being savings bank assets, have also risen steadily. The general government funds held with the Crown Agents include development reserves held against planned development expenditures and working balances for current expenditure. The other funds which are held with United Kingdom banks represent the general banking assets of commercial banks operating in the Colonies and known liquid funds held in London of companies and individuals resident there.

(ii) *Independent Sterling Area Holdings*

11. It is the normal practice of central banks in independent sterling area countries to hold the bulk of their foreign exchange reserves in the form of sterling. Moreover they are often required by statute to hold certain minimum reserves in foreign exchange (which may include sterling) against local currency issues. A large proportion of these statutory reserves are in practice held in sterling.

(iii) *Holdings of Non-sterling Countries*

12. Most of the sterling held by non-sterling countries is now in the nature of working balances required to finance commercial transactions. The holdings of central banks in O.E.E.C. countries are influenced by the operation of the European Payments Union, to which further reference is made in paragraph 20 (1) below.

(iv) *Holdings of Non-territorial Organisations*

13. The holdings of non-territorial organisations are in a special category, and are for some purposes best excluded from the total of the sterling liabilities. The two main holders are the International Monetary Fund (I.M.F.) and the International Bank for Reconstruction and Development (I.B.R.D.). At the end of 1957, out of £645 million held by all non-territorial organisations, the I.M.F. held £583 million. This holding arises partly from the original United Kingdom subscription to the Fund, and partly represents the sterling paid in exchange for dollar drawings at the end of 1956. The I.B.R.D. held £55 million at the end of 1957. This consisted principally of the original subscription, which is being gradually drawn down as sterling loans are made by the I.B.R.D. to other member countries. The remaining £7 million was held by various international organisations, e.g. the Bank for International Settlements.

14. *Analysis by class and term of holding.* It will be seen that all the funds included in the series are highly liquid, in that they are either very short-dated or, normally, easily realisable in the market; and that almost all are liabilities of the British Government or of banking offices in the United Kingdom. The Government issues range from Treasury Bills falling due within a few days to stocks maturing many years hence, and some irredeemable stocks are included. This does not mean that the funds will be held for these varying periods of time. Deposits, though fluctuating from day to day, may be maintained at approximately the same level indefinitely; Treasury Bills may be renewed again and again; and on the other hand longer-

dated securities may be realised in cash through the stock markets for immediate spending. It follows that a division of holdings as a whole into what is short-term or long-term in form gives no sure indication of the ratio of volatile to stable funds; though special funds (e.g. pension funds) are naturally invested in types of security appropriate to their purposes.

15. No detailed classification is available of the form in which the net balances with commercial banks are held. *Ad hoc* investigations have however been made at intervals into the composition of the holdings of central banks and other official agencies. At 31 December 1956, of these holdings[1] approximately 8 per cent consisted of bank deposits, 32 per cent of Treasury Bills and 60 per cent of British Government securities. The Government securities showed the following distribution by maturity.

Years to final date of redemption	Percentage of total
Not over 5	47
Over 5 but not over 10	15
Over 10 but not over 15	24
Over 15	14

16. *Post-war trends in sterling holdings.* In the middle of 1939 United Kingdom net external liabilities amounted to rather more than £500 million. During the war years overseas sterling holdings rose extremely fast and at the end of 1945 stood at approaching £3,600 million.

Of this total a large proportion represented obligations to other countries arising from the exigencies of war, rather than their working balances or normal reserves voluntarily held in London. (For a general account of the growth of the balances the reader may be referred to Professor Sayers' *Financial Policy 1939–45* in the Civil Histories of the Second World War, published by H.M.S.O., 1956.)

17. The level of holdings for each year since the end of the war by areas is shown in Table III. It will be seen that there have been striking changes in the distribution of the balances:

[1] Excluding non-territorial organisations.

£ million

OVERSEAS STERLING HOLDINGS	1945	1946	1947	1948	1949	1950	1951	1952	1953	1954	1955	1956	1957
Sterling area countries													
United Kingdom Colonies	411	461	470	519	546	719	919	1,024	1,093	1,221	1,280	1,281	1,269
Other sterling area countries	1,986	1,906	1,780	1,636	1,612	1,830	1,717	1,518	1,705	1,703	1,599	1,575	1,430
Total sterling area countries	2,397	2,367	2,250	2,155	2,158	2,549	2,636	2,542	2,798	2,924	2,879	2,856	2,699
Non-sterling countries													
Dollar area	34	33	18	19	31	79	38	34	62	97	58	37	35
Other western hemisphere	163	212	235	135	80	45	57	6	40	8	9	32	31
O.E.E.C. countries	351	363	419	309	356	314	328	239	223	244	213	193	258
Other non-sterling countries	622	635	576	534	518	496	518	398	370	430	417	303	244
Total non-sterling countries	1,170	1,243	1,248	997	985	934	941	677	695	779	697	565	568
Total—All countries	3,567	3,610	3,498	3,152	3,143	3,483	3,577	3,219	3,493	3,703	3,576	3,421	3,267
Non-territorial organisations	—	26	388	398	576	577	566	567	511	476	469	669	645
Total	3,567	3,636	3,886	3,550	3,719	4,060	4,143	3,786	4,004	4,179	4,045	4,090	3,912
ACCEPTANCES OUTSTANDING	..	..	30	53	50	71	92	70	69	102	101	126	147

the colonial balances being trebled over the twelve years, those of independent sterling countries being reduced by a quarter, and those of non-sterling countries being halved.

18. The composition of the increased sterling holdings of the colonial territories during the post-war years has already been briefly described. The underlying reason for the growth of this total was the expansion of colonial economies at a time of rising prices. An important special factor was the unprecedentedly high level of colonial export earnings in the years following the outbreak of the Korean War. More recently the colonial territories have been in deficit on current account, but as there has also been a large capital inflow there has been little change in the general level of sterling holdings.

19. Much of the fall in the holdings of independent sterling area countries took place in the first few years after the war, and represented the reduction of surplus balances built up during the war years. During the last few years trends in individual countries have been diverse. Among the major changes, India's holding has recently been run down further to finance the second five-year development plan, and the holdings of Australia and New Zealand have fluctuated widely, largely under the influence of changes in the prices of their exports of primary products and import policies. On the other hand, the balances of the Middle East sterling area countries have increased considerably.

20. The holdings of non-sterling countries can be divided into three groups—those of O.E.E.C. countries, those of dollar countries, and those of other non-sterling countries.

(1) Since 1950 the trend of the holdings of O.E.E.C. countries has been much influenced by the workings of The European Payments Union (E.P.U.) mechanism. The E.P.U. Agreement provided that central banks of the countries participating should treat certain defined holdings of sterling in excess of working balances at 30 June 1950 as 'existing resources', which could be used in settlement of current deficits with the Union. Part of the fall of £75 million in O.E.E.C. countries' holdings between 1950 and 1952 was due to the running down of these 'existing re-

sources'. Since then the central bank holdings of sterling by
O.E.E.C. countries have been small. To this, however,
there are two exceptions.

(a) Under the workings of E.P.U. the sterling holdings of
member countries' central banks, reflecting transactions
during the month, are reported to the Agent at the end
of each month for inclusion in the calculation of surpluses and deficits. When these surpluses or deficits are
settled during the following month, partly in gold or
dollars and partly by changes in E.P.U. debit or credit,
these 'reported' sterling holdings are adjusted accordingly. They thus distort the trend in the total of sterling
holdings of O.E.E.C. countries and are therefore distinguished in the new quarterly series.

(b) There are special holdings by the German authorities:
an arms purchase account established by deposits of
£20 million in September 1956 and £10 million in
April 1957, and a special deposit of £75 million, largely
made in the third quarter of 1957 from which annual
repayments of post-war debt due from the German
Government are being made. These deposits were
mainly responsible for the rise in O.E.E.C. countries'
holdings in 1957.

Allowance made for these complications, the holdings of
O.E.E.C. countries nowadays represent sterling held by
residents of these countries for commercial and financial
reasons and their size will vary with the scale of the holders'
business in sterling and their judgment of the attractiveness
of London as a financial centre in which to hold funds (and
also, since the figures are net of overdrafts, etc., to borrow
on short term).

(2) The same generalisation is applicable to the habitually small
net balances of sterling held by dollar area countries.

(3) The very large fall (over £500 million) in the holdings of
other non-sterling countries since the war was due to the
fact that several of these countries had accumulated large
holdings of sterling, well beyond what they needed for commercial purposes, during the war period. Egypt was an out-

standing example of this, and in this and some other such cases the funds were transferred to special accounts, commonly called 'blocked', and provision made for annual releases. Apart from these special accumulations, which have now been mainly used up, most of the countries in this group (including countries in the Far East, Middle East, Western Hemisphere and Soviet bloc) only hold sterling funds for the normal purpose of financing their foreign trade, particularly with sterling area countries.

21. *Seasonal movements in sterling holdings.* There are marked seasonal variations in the earnings of individual sterling area countries and these differ in size and incidence from country to country. When aggregated to give the earnings of the rest of the sterling area as a whole some seasonal movement remains and this is reflected in the sterling balances which constitute their principal foreign exchange reserves. During the last four years the quarterly changes in sterling holdings of countries in the independent sterling area and of the colonial territories have been as follows:

Changes in sterling holdings

	1st qtr.	2nd qtr.	3rd qtr.	4th qtr.	Year
	£ million				
Colonial territories					
1954	+51	+39	+30	+8	+128
1955	+37	+35	—10	—3	+59
1956	+22	—1	+4	—24	+1
1957	+28	—	—29	—11	—12
Other sterling area					
1954	+47	—11	—74	+36	—2
1955	—48	—12	—69	+25	—104
1956	+3	—3	—13	—11	—24
1957	+33	+8	—107	—79	—145
Total sterling area					
1954	+98	+28	—44	+44	+126
1955	—11	+23	—79	+22	—45
1956	+25	—4	—9	—35	—23
1957	+61	+8	—136	—90	—157

This net movement can, however, vary considerably from year to year. In the last two years the seasonal pattern has been affected by the closing of the Suez Canal at the end of 1956 and by Indian I.M.F. drawings in the first two quarters of 1957. However, in normal years the most difficult period for overseas sterling area countries as a whole tends to be concentrated in the third quarter.

22. There is no such seasonal pattern in the holdings of non-sterling countries, for movements here depend on quite different factors. The quarterly changes have been as follows:

	1st qtr.	2nd qtr.	3rd qtr.	4th qtr.	Year
			£ million		
1954	—67	+65	+38	+48	+84
1955	+42	—66	—37	—21	—82
1956	—33	—15	—36	—48	—132
1957	+3	+1	+11	—12	+3

23. *Acceptances outstanding*. This series,[1] which is now published for the first time, represents the total of sterling acceptances given by banking offices in the United Kingdom for account of residents abroad and outstanding at the dates shown. These acceptances are reimbursable by non-residents of the United Kingdom not later than the date of maturity of the accepted bill. Acceptances for which funds have been specifically provided and segregated are excluded so that the amounts shown represent claims on other countries (very largely outside the sterling area) additional to those types of asset which have been deducted in calculating overseas sterling holdings.

24. Credit taken in the United Kingdom by the rest of the world has developed since the war in line with the increased value of international trade, and in particular with certain types of trade; and certain countries have used this kind of facility much more than others. Seasonal movements too are discernible, corresponding with the movement of goods, especially raw materials exported from the sterling area to countries

[1] Table in the paper as originally published has here been omitted. The figures are given in the Balance of Payments White Paper.

outside the sterling area, for which financing by bank acceptance is important. Various methods of financing transactions are open to traders, whose choice is influenced by the existing level of interest rates and expectations about future developments. Moreover the giving of credit to residents outside the sterling area is subject to Exchange Control, and there have been from time to time changes in the regulations governing the types of arrangement which are permissible.

III MONETARY POSITION

25. The overseas sterling holdings constitute a fairly comprehensive measure of the sterling resources readily at the disposal of the rest of the world. As the preceding discussion has shown, a substantial part of them is held for long-term purposes and may legitimately be regarded as permanent or semi-permanent investment in the United Kingdom.[1] Were this component clearly defined, changes in it could in principle be best treated as long-term investment or disinvestment in the United Kingdom. But, with this reservation, changes in overseas sterling holdings may be regarded as 'financing items' of the same general kind as the other items, viz., changes in reserves, E.P.U. debt, etc., with which they are grouped in the tables of recent White Papers on the balance of payments.

26. Because the countries of the rest of the sterling area hold the bulk of their external reserves in sterling, changes in their holdings by and large reflect their surplus or deficit on all transactions with the rest of the world, i.e. with the United Kingdom as well as with the non-sterling world. These transactions will include short-term and miscellaneous capital as well as current and long-term capital transactions. Changes arising out of their direct transactions with the United Kingdom are shown in items 1–15 (*a*, *b* and *c*) in Table 2 of the White Papers.

[1] Because the coverage of the sterling holdings (liabilities) is thus so much wider than that of the assets shown in the published statistics (the Exchange Equalisation Account's holdings of gold and dollars, and other non-sterling currencies), the *absolute* difference between these aggregates gives an unduly unfavourable picture of the United Kingdom's *absolute* position on international account. As these paragraphs explain, it is *changes* in this difference over time that are significant, rather than the difference itself at any one moment.

Their net receipts arising in settlement of their transactions with the non-sterling world (whether in sterling or in other currencies) and from their sales of gold, are shown in the same table as items 21–22, under the description 'inter-area transfers'.[1]

27. The sterling holdings of non-sterling countries, as has been pointed out, consist for the most part of balances held for commercial and financial reasons; they are primarily working balances rather than, as in the case of the countries of the rest of the sterling area, working balances plus national reserves of foreign exchange and other official funds. They are to a considerable extent convertible into gold or dollars: American account and Registered sterling having full convertibility, and Transferable sterling in the hands of central banks being partially available for conversion through the mechanism of E.P.U. settlements and other holdings through the transferable sterling markets. Thus though the sterling receipts or payments of non-sterling countries over a period will depend largely on their balance of payments with sterling area countries in the aggregate, the amount of sterling which people in those countries will retain on their accounts is a matter almost entirely at their discretion.

28. Three general conclusions follow from this. First, the net change in any period in the total of all overseas sterling holdings, the reserves, acceptances and the other financing items, reflect the United Kingdom's overall balance on current account and long-term and any other capital transactions not covered by the overseas sterling holdings series itself.[2] But separate factors influ-

[1] As a net R.S.A. receipt of sterling from non-sterling countries tends to increase United Kingdom liabilities to the R.S.A., it appears with a negative sign in Table 2. Conversely the same sterling transfer from the non-sterling world reduces United Kingdom liabilities to that area and is shown in Table 3 (describing the United Kingdom balance of payments with the non-sterling area) with a positive sign.

[2] 'Long-term capital' includes transactions undertaken in order to strengthen the exchange position, such as the borrowing from the United States Export/Import Bank last year. A drawing from the International Monetary Fund by the United Kingdom will tend to increase reserves but will also increase liabilities (i.e. the sterling holdings of the International Monetary Fund) and so will not affect the overall balance as here defined. A drawing from the International Monetary Fund by another country in the sterling area in so far as it strengthens the central reserves, directly or indirectly, to that extent tends to increase sterling holdings of the rest of the sterling area. It therefore improves the overall balance vis-a-vis non-sterling countries. In all these cases a liability to repay gold or dollars is being built up.

ence the individual items. Second, the net changes in sterling holdings of non-sterling countries, less acceptances re-imbursable by them, less reserves and other non-sterling currencies, plus the United Kingdom debit in E.P.U., measure the corresponding balance of the whole sterling area, and not that of the United Kingdom alone. (The contributions of the United Kingdom and the rest of the sterling area are statistically distinguishable in Table 3 of the Balance of Payments White Papers: items 1–15 showing the United Kingdom's contribution and items 21 and 22, the inter-area transfers, showing the rest of the sterling area's.)

29. Thirdly, this analysis emphasises the extent to which movements in the gold and dollar reserves, though naturally of great importance, do not in themselves in any simple way reflect the United Kingdom's current, or current and long-term capital, balance of payments. They are but one indication of the whole complex of the relations of the United Kingdom and the rest of the sterling area with the non-sterling world. A full understanding of them requires a study of the whole web of statistics shown in the six-monthly White Papers.

Overseas Holdings of Sterling[1]

(Memorandum submitted by the Bank of England to the Radcliffe Committee. Source: *Principal Memoranda of Evidence*, Vol. I)

1. An important feature of the British monetary system is the volume of sterling (or liquid claims to sterling) held by, or for account of, overseas holders.

2. At the outset it is necessary to make clear how far this volume of sterling is identifiable and measurable. The Bank of England compile figures of overseas sterling holdings from confidential returns made by banks, currency authorities, Crown Agents, etc. These figures are loosely referred to as 'sterling balances'; but in fact the funds comprise cash, funds employed at short-term in the London Money Market, bills of exchange, particularly Treasury Bills, and securities predominantly of the

---

[1] See Minutes of Evidence Qns. 948 to 971.

British Government and mainly (but not entirely) of short or short-medium date. The figures do not include commercial indebtedness outstanding, direct investment in the United Kingdom, nor security investments other than those (mainly Government securities) held by or for overseas Governments and banking offices. They are balances struck at a point of time and take no account of contracts not yet matured.[1]

3. On the other hand, the nature of the reporting institutions indicates that, in whatever form they may be held, the funds are primarily liquid resources in the hands of their ultimate owners, held as working balances, as reserves against local currency, or against future liabilities to be discharged in sterling. Not all the funds will ever be required at the same time; some of them are held against liabilities well in the future, e.g. accruing pension funds and sinking funds on sterling Colonial loans are held by the Crown Agents. But movements in them depend on whether the owners—for their own reasons—are adding to or drawing on their working balances and reserves; and secondly whether—given the level of their working balances and reserves—they decide to keep a larger or smaller proportion of them in another currency or in gold instead of sterling.

4. The holders themselves may be roughly divided into the following four groups:

A. Countries outside the sterling area.
B. Independent Commonwealth Countries (plus the Irish Republic, Iceland and Burma).
C. Colonial territories, including those becoming Independent.
D. The Middle East.

A. COUNTRIES OUTSIDE THE STERLING AREA

5. At the end of the last war, many of these countries held more sterling than they wanted. By the end of 1956, their

---

[1] The figures given below in this paper differ from the series published in Balance of Payments White Papers by including, in addition, sterling securities issued by Dominions or Colonies and held with the Crown Agents for Oversea Governments and Administrations and by Currency Boards and (to a small extent) by other official bodies.

holdings seem to have been reduced to a natural (perhaps low) working level—except for the £128 million of Egypt (a special case) and the debtor position of the United Kingdom in the European Payments Union of £125 million of which almost the whole will be paid off under consolidation agreements over the next four to eight years. At any rate the pressure on sterling in December 1956 left the total (£570 million)[1] only £5 million down on the month, and subsequently there has been some increase. It is not from these quarters that further major and continuing problems are most likely to arise.

B. Independent Commonwealth, etc. Countries

6. This group comprises Australia, New Zealand, South Africa, India, Pakistan, Ceylon, Rhodesia, Irish Republic, Iceland and Burma. Each of these countries has a monetary system of its own. Only Australia, New Zealand, Ceylon, Iceland and India (up to a certain point) are free to meet local currency needs without having to maintain a minimum relationship between them and the reserves. With the exception of Ceylon, Burma and Rhodesia, each holds some gold in its monetary reserves, that in South Africa being the main reserve. Sterling is held as a convenient external reserve although in most cases sterling is not specifically mentioned as the reserve currency. The holding of any one country in this group can fall to a level regarded by that country as a minimum, having in mind its own external needs and the internal difficulties of righting an external deficit.

7. These countries have, with fluctuations, reduced their total holdings from £1,777 million at the end of 1950 to £1,260 million at the end of 1956. None, with the exception of India, whose holdings have fallen markedly during the past year, now holds sterling much in excess of a reasonable minimum. The main problem set by these countries for the United Kingdom is the impact of fluctuations in their external position as reflected in changes in their holdings of sterling; the recent large fall, and subsequent rise, in Australian holdings is a case in point. The more synchronised these fluctuations the greater the problem.

[1] Excluding the £125 million in E.P.U.

But, apart from a further reduction in the Indian balances in connection with development programmes, no great fall in the aggregate holdings of this group need be looked for, given the continuance of reasonably prosperous international trading conditions.

C. Colonial Territories

8. During the last five years, the internal volume of currency and bank money in the Colonies has greatly increased, with a corresponding increase in sterling cover. Between 31 December 1950 and 31 December 1956 Currency Board funds and currency funds held by the Crown Agents have risen by £182 million to £464 million, and sterling held by the Colonies with United Kingdom banks by £58 million to £250 million. In the same period the reserve funds of Colonial Governments and Marketing Board funds rose by £406 million to £740 million. Some two-thirds of this last total was held for West Africa, Malaya and Singapore. Over the six years the total of reported Colonial holdings rose from £808 million to £1,454 million.

9. The combination of high commodity prices, rising monetary circulation, conservative government finance and the provision of new capital for development mainly from United Kingdom sources, both governmental and private, has thus resulted in a total of sterling holdings for the colonial group now larger than that of the Independent Commonwealth group.

10. For various reasons, not least because important colonial areas have reached or are reaching independent status, the picture is changing; the growth in colonial sterling holdings had virtually come to a halt in 1956.

11. First, all important Colonies are now at liberty to substitute local securities for at least 20 per cent of the sterling backing of their note issue. As local currency requirements rise, larger total monetary reserves will be needed, with the result that, despite larger fiduciary issues (which are not yet being urgently pressed), the absolute amount of sterling held in the reserves may not be much lower; but if the total of sterling backing does not fall, its rate of increase may be expected at least to fall away.

12. Secondly, recent consultations between the Colonies and H.M. Government on development envisage that development schemes which have been set in train in recent years are likely to call for expenditure during the next three years at about one and a half times the recent rate. In view of the likely difficulty of meeting more than a small part of this expenditure by way of loans or grants the pressure to draw on sterling holdings will be increased.

13. Thirdly, there is likely to be a continuing trend towards higher imports for consumption; this would put a further strain on the sterling resources of the Colonies.

14. Over a period, the aggregate effect of these factors could lead to substantial drawings on the sterling holdings of this group, particularly on those which represent general reserve funds or Marketing Board funds.

D. THE MIDDLE EAST

15. This is mainly a story of oil. Sterling held by Iraq, Jordan, Libya and the Persian Gulf Territories rose from £71 million at the end of 1950 to £338 million at the end of 1956. It will continue to grow as long as oil royalties accrue and are held or invested in sterling faster than local development is taking place.

16. Thus the four groups show to some extent different tendencies; and it is noteworthy how far their movements offset each other during the six years 1951/56:

	(£ Million)
Group A—'Non-Sterling' Countries	—369
B—Independent Commonwealth	—517
C—Colonial	+646
D—Middle East	+267
Net	+27

In addition a net £205 million was, in effect, borrowed from the European Payments Union. The economy of the United Kingdom was not unaffected by these large movements, but their offsetting character reduced the strain.

17. Looking ahead, the first group may not change much

either way; the second is likely to fluctuate; the third may well fall appreciably; it would be rash to count on the fourth as an adequate stabiliser. These suggestions rest on the assumption of reasonably fair weather in economic conditions over the world as a whole. If in the interplay of trade and payments which is settled in London, sterling released by one overseas holder is not absorbed by another, it must be absorbed by a United Kingdom resident or add to the demand upon the gold and exchange reserves. If the latter is to be avoided, a continuous effort will be required, in the form of an export surplus; and a continuing export surplus would, in turn, have important consequences both for the control of inflation at home and for the amount of savings available for investment programmes here or overseas— since an increase in the reserves or a reduction of overseas liabilities are themselves forms of investment which call for, and absorb, savings.

18. There would also be important market consequences. The overseas holdings that may be run down are predominantly in Treasury Bills or in gilt-edged securities. If the former, then the task of maintaining market Floating Debt within manageable limits is made more difficult. If the latter, then the volume of sales (which may include some securities of Commonwealth borrowers) represents as much of a strain on the capacity of the gilt-edged market as an equivalent amount of new securities, including those of or guaranteed by H.M. Government.

19. It is not practicable to put any figures on these possibilities; but the existence of these balances represents a potential call on the current savings and on the reserves of the United Kingdom. Thus they are extremely relevant both to the size of what can be found for long-term lending or for grants to the Commonwealth or the rest of the world; and also to the size of investment programmes at home.

III

POLICY PROBLEMS

(i) *Monetary Policy and External Economic Problems*

(Memorandum submitted by H.M. Treasury to the Radcliffe Committee. Source: *Principal Memoranda of Evidence*, Vol. I)

I INTRODUCTION

1. The United Kingdom is a great international trader, a large source and recipient of international flows of long-term capital, and the possessor of a currency the use of which in vast sums abroad can give rise to large short-term movements. Our economic affairs and those of the outside world are thus closely linked in these three separate ways. Hence the problems which arise over our external balance (whether they start from home or foreign causes) must profoundly affect our monetary policy and such policy itself must affect the success or failure with which we deal with our external problems.

2. This paper seeks to provide a broad general analysis of the range of questions which arise from these facts. Part II sets out the major facts of the external position, draws the main conclusions for policy from them, and describes the environment within which policy has to be conducted. Part III comes back to the same nexus of questions from another angle; and tries to set out the main ways in which monetary policy operates upon the various elements of the balance of payments.

II THE MAJOR EXTERNAL FACTORS

3. The very general description of the United Kingdom's external financial relationships given above can be made rather more precise, for the purposes of the present memorandum, by recording and commenting upon three major factors:

(*a*) The status of sterling as an international currency.

(*b*) Long-term investment overseas.

(*c*) The present relationship between our external monetary assets and liabilities.

4. The background to this discussion is that, by deliberate decision of Government policy enshrined in international obligation, the sterling exchange rate is fixed in terms of gold and the dollar, and is kept by the action of the Exchange Equalisation Account within a 1 per cent margin of the 2·80 dollars parity.

5. In addition it may be useful to the understanding of the problems dealt with in this paper to explain the reasons why the United Kingdom does not apply exchange control to transactions with R.S.A. (Rest of the Sterling Area) countries. The local monetary systems of R.S.A. countries are ultimately based on London as their centre of liquidity where funds can be lodged or withdrawn at will. To interpose an exchange control between the centre of liquidity and the local monetary systems which are based on it would not merely raise formidable administrative difficulties between the London offices of banks and their branches, subsidiaries or associates in the other sterling countries, but would threaten one of the fundamental features of the sterling system. This was accepted as a decisive consideration when exchange control was imposed on transactions with the non-sterling world in 1939 and, as the London balances of sterling countries continued to grow during the war, was reinforced by a further consideration, namely, that if a barrier of United Kingdom controls were set between London and the other sterling countries they would be under growing incentive to reduce their funds in London. In more recent years, the policy of successive United Kingdom Governments on Commonwealth development has provided yet another reason for allowing freedom for commercial enterprises to develop their businesses in what is their traditional field—this private direct investment being the largest single overseas contributor to development in the R.S.A. This freedom to invest is but another facet of the general principle of freedom of access to the United Kingdom by R.S.A. countries in trade and finance on which the sterling system was founded and has developed. From the outset, the 'ring fence' of

the exchange controls which all members of the sterling area maintain on transactions with the non-sterling world was relied on to prevent the freedom to move funds from the United Kingdom to other parts of the area being used to cover payments outside the area.

The Status of Sterling as an International Currency

6. Sterling as an international currency has two characteristics. It is a *reserve* currency for the countries of the rest of the sterling area, and it is a *trading* currency both for them and for a great part of the non-sterling world. For both reasons it is held in large quantities by other countries. As explained in the memorandum on 'The Sterling Area' (p. 33, *supra*) sterling funds held by the R.S.A. and those held by the N.S.A. (non-sterling area) are subject to fluctuations for somewhat different reasons:

(a) R.S.A. sterling holdings are liable to change mainly in a manner that reflects the overall balance of payments, on current and long-term capital account, of the countries concerned. While there may also be some ebb and flow of short-term sterling funds to and from London, holdings of gold and non-sterling currencies by R.S.A. countries are, generally speaking, extremely stable. This accords with the fundamental features of the sterling area discussed in the memorandum referred to.

(b) But in the N.S.A. countries these features are not present, and therefore N.S.A. sterling holdings are liable to be switched at short notice into gold or other currencies. American Account sterling and registered sterling[1] are formally convertible. The third category of externally-held sterling, transferable sterling, can also be directly converted, at a small discount, in the transferable market. While the movements in these balances of course take place largely for reasons connected with the current trade

---

[1] 'Registered sterling' is sterling standing to the credit of a 'registered account' in the name of a person resident outside the Scheduled Territories, the American Account Area and Canada, which has been acquired by the sale of gold or U.S. or Canadian dollars or by transfer from an American, Canadian or other 'registered account'.

of the countries concerned, they can and do also move rapidly for non-trading reasons, arising from 'confidence', changes in short-term interest rates, etc.

7. Equally the position of London as an international monetary centre involves short-term lending both to the R.S.A. and, subject to exchange control supervision, to the N.S.A. as well. This lending is an integral part of the services of a monetary centre, and takes the various forms of bank overdrafts, acceptance credits and so on.

Long-term Investment Overseas

8. Because there is no exchange control between the United Kingdom and the R.S.A. and because the countries of the R.S.A. have traditionally looked to the United Kingdom as a major source of external capital, there has been in all post-war years a large net outflow of long-term capital to them subjected, broadly, only to the same controls over new borrowing that are applied to domestic borrowers. Commonwealth development has been an important theme in this country's post-war policy. (See, for example, paragraphs 9–14 of the Final Communiqué of the Commonwealth Economic Conference of December 1952, Cmd. 8717.) Besides its political importance in linking the Commonwealth countries together, this investment is a major economic interest for the United Kingdom, developing new resources of vital importance to our economy and building up existing overseas assets. Long-term investment outside the sterling area is subject to exchange control and has had to be restricted by special criteria. Permissions have principally been granted for investment in Canada and in the oil industry; types of investment to which the same general considerations of policy and interest apply as in the case of R.S.A. investment. The net capital outflow under these headings is of considerable importance in determining balance of payments policy, and is influenced by the general policy towards investment, in which monetary policy plays a part.

The Relationship between Monetary Assets and Liabilities

9. Figures on this subject have been given in the Treasury

memorandum on 'The Sterling Area'. Though, as there pointed out, the available statistical series do not permit any exact measurement of the balance of monetary assets and liabilities, itself a concept not easy to define precisely, there can be no doubt that on any reckoning our monetary liabilities exceed our monetary assets by a substantial margin. In other words our reserves are, and have been since the end of the war, altogether too small in relation to our needs.

10. These three major factors of our external monetary position (the status of sterling as an international currency, long-term investment overseas, and the relationship between our monetary assets and liabilities) of necessity give rise to two dominant objectives in external policy:

(*a*) the maintenance of confidence in sterling, and

(*b*) the earning of an adequate external surplus.

The Necessity for Confidence

11. The present relationship between reserves and overseas sterling holdings would alone make it vital that confidence in sterling should be maintained. As already pointed out, the balances of sterling area holders are not liable to be converted into gold or non-sterling currencies for speculative or short-term reasons. But this fundamental feature of the sterling system is in fact based on confidence which has to be maintained by United Kingdom policy and needs to be continually refreshed. The performance of R.S.A. countries in this respect in post-war years has derived from a sense of common interest and a belief in the determination of the United Kingdom Government to achieve sound conditions.

12. The sterling holdings of N.S.A. countries, as the trend of the figures sufficiently shows, are by contrast liable to sharp fluctuations for confidence reasons, and movements in them have for long been a major cause of reserve changes. In aggregate these holdings are now substantially reduced, but a large-scale withdrawal could still precipitate a serious crisis.

13. A withdrawal of sterling by overseas holders is not the only threat to the external position and the exchange rate which can arise for confidence reasons. The complex of phenomena

known as 'leads and lags' can be equally serious, and, of course, these tend to occur precisely at times when overseas funds may be being run down. To give traders a proper freedom in their daily business, exchange control in the United Kingdom does not interfere with the timing of payments or receipts within a six-month limit, and there is therefore some 'play' around the normal relationship between contract and payment. With a monthly turnover of current trade between the sterling area and the non-sterling world of the order of £1,000 million, it is obvious that only a very small acceleration of payments or delay in receipts can have a large effect upon reserves. In consequence a widespread and persistent expectation of a change in the exchange rate, however ill-based in the first place, can produce reserve movements on a scale which begins to give much more solid grounds for the initial expectation. This is all the more difficult in that there can be no means of precisely identifying the emergence of 'leads and lags'; a fall in sterling balances is quickly recorded, but when a small shift in the timing of payments and receipts occurs, it cannot be distinguished from a genuine swing in the current balance until some time has passed.

14. The confidence which it thus becomes all the more essential to maintain is not only that of residents of non-sterling countries, or even of them and R.S.A. residents alone. The confidence of the trading community in this country is equally involved, especially, of course, in respect of *payments* for imports, but also to some extent because it affects the *volume* of imports. If a reduction in the exchange rate is expected it is not only a matter of commercial prudence to pay for imports quickly; but it becomes sensible also, at least in some cases, actually to increase the volume of imports, anticipating future purchases which might otherwise become more costly in terms of sterling. Nor is it a matter of current transactions only. When the confidence of residents is shaken there is a strong incentive to invest in non-sterling securities or to increase cash balances in non-sterling currencies. While exchange control can very largely inhibit, it cannot be expected completely to prevent capital movements of this kind at times of speculative pressure.

F

15. Finally, it should be noted that confidence is largely a relative term. Expectations of the appreciation of some other important currency can have immediate effects upon the reserves very much akin to those of expectations of devaluation of sterling. Experience in the third quarter of 1957 has demonstrated this.

The Necessity for an Adequate External Surplus

16. As a precondition for the maintenance of external and internal confidence, and in order to meet both contractual and other commitments, it is essential that the United Kingdom should earn an adequate balance of payments surplus on current account. The current account, as defined in White Papers on the United Kingdom Balance of Payments, includes payments in respect of net Government military and civil expenditure overseas, and the interest on Government overseas debt (mainly the United States and Canadian loans). Other transactions in the current account must therefore yield a sufficient net receipt to cover these payments. But for them to do no more than this, i.e. for the current account to be merely in balance, would be wholly insufficient. To prevent a call on the reserves (other things being equal) a surplus is needed to cover:

(a) Private net long-term capital outflow, and

(b) The capital repayments of Government overseas debt, as well as

(c) Net Government long-term lending overseas.

The sum of the above factors may be described as the 'balance of current and long-term capital transactions', a concept which distinguishes our trading and investing roles from our role as an international banker. This balance must itself be in surplus if our overseas monetary position, i.e. the balance of our overseas monetary assets and liabilities, is to be strengthened. This position can be improved either by reducing liabilities or by increasing assets. Liabilities are reduced when the R.S.A. or N.S.A. countries run down their sterling balances, and this follows from their own decisions of policy. But such reductions will fall upon our reserves unless we have a surplus on current and long-term capital account sufficient to offset this. But if in addition to covering a reduction of liabilities we are also to increase the reserves, so as to make them more adequate to our needs, we must secure a surplus yet greater than that required to offset the factors already enumerated.

17. These factors are not for the most part constant or easy to forecast. In aggregate they can vary very much from year to year. It is only practicable to obtain a broad judgment of the average balance of payments surplus on current account which is desirable year-in year-out over the years immediately ahead, and then, in the daily evolution of policy, seek decisions that will both make a contribution towards the average in the next short period, and assist the creation of the right setting for further contributions in the longer term. In the Economic Survey for 1953, paragraphs 101–4, there were published some calculations leading to an average 'requirement' of £300–350 million. In fact achievement in 1953/56 fell substantially short of this target, and we have subsequently had to incur further overseas commitments on medium-term capital account, to strengthen our short-term position—the £200 million I.M.F. drawing of December 1956 and the October 1957 borrowing from the United States Export-Import Bank.

18. The general conclusion that can be drawn from this section of the paper is that these facts of the external position necessarily limit our freedom in our general economic policies, including monetary policy. The consequences of a failure to achieve the external objectives we set ourselves, even by small amounts, can have disproportionate effects on the whole economy. It is therefore all the more important that we should not take risks in the management of the domestic economy of a kind that affect the balance of payments.

III Monetary Policy and the Balance of Payments

19. An earlier memorandum (paper No. 6) discusses the role of monetary policy in the control of economic conditions as a whole. In this external problems have been covered generally as part of the wider question and the present section attempts to provide a further analysis in the light of the assessment just given of the external background.

20. As in the principal paper the discussion centres on the role of monetary policy as distinct from the two other categories of policy there distinguished; direct interventions and fiscal policy. But something must first be said about the special place of one of the former in balance of payments policy: namely exchange control.

21. *Exchange Control.* A very stringent apparatus of controls over current and capital transactions with non-sterling countries was developed under the stress of war. Exchange control continues to play today an important part in external policy and is the responsibility of the Treasury, who delegate certain powers to the Bank of England.

22. As already explained in paragraph 5 above, exchange control is not applied to transactions with the sterling area. Exchange control upon transactions with the non-sterling world works in two main ways:

(*a*) United Kingdom residents can make payments on current or capital account to non-residents only for authorised purposes.

(*b*) It requires repatriation of the proceeds of trade and sets conditions upon the type of foreign currency and the source of the sterling that can be accepted in payment. It controls the amounts of non-sterling currencies which residents may hold and of credit which they may give.

23. The severity of the control imposed has varied from time to time, but the general trend of policy has been towards relaxation. Thus, for example, it was stated in paragraph 20 of the final communiqué of the Commonwealth Economic Conference, December 1952 (Cmd. 8717) that the United Kingdom, with other Commonwealth countries, 'agreed that it is important, not only for the United Kingdom and the sterling area but also for the world, that sterling should resume its full role as a medium of world trade and exchange'. Moreover, the United Kingdom has commitments to the International Monetary Fund, the G.A.T.T. and O.E.E.C. to seek the freeing of trade and payments.

24. Within its limits exchange control is still strict and effective. But for practical administration and to meet the require-

ments of efficient trade, some latitude has to be given, and, as already pointed out in paragraph 13 above, considerable 'confidence' movements remain possible. Exchange control cannot be regarded as a substitute for general economic policy; it can be no more than an adjunct.

25. The remainder of this paper is devoted to a discussion of the effects of monetary policy upon the balance of payments. As is pointed out, however, in the earlier memorandum, monetary policy is only one of the instruments used by the Government to influence general economic conditions. Hence it is impossible to make a quantitative estimate of the separate influence on the external position of monetary policy alone; only broad qualitative judgments can be made.

Monetary Policy and the Current Balance of Payments

26. For the present purposes it is convenient to distinguish four separate balances:

(a) The balance of goods and services.

(b) The balance of income and expenditure from property (roughly, interest, profits, dividends, though including also remittances which represent the contribution of branches and subsidiaries to the current expenses of headquarters, etc., in the United Kingdom).

(c) The balance of Government transactions (Government current expenditure overseas, and such receipts as Defence Aid).

(d) The balance of current transfers—migrants' funds, legacies, etc.

Of these (c) will of course be primarily determined by the Government itself, and, as pointed out in paragraph 28 of the earlier memorandum, will be influenced by its general assessment of the economy rather than by monetary policy itself; (d) is small; and only the first two balances are examined here. Table I shows the four balances for the last eleven years.

27. The *Goods and Services balance* depends on the contending pressures of economic conditions at home and overseas and is the sector of the balance of payments which reflects most closely the shifts in the general state of trade in the home and world

economies. While the Government may seek to influence economic conditions in the outside world, in the short run its policies must take account of these conditions as they in fact exist. Hence, if the interaction of external conditions and the position of the home economy is such as to produce an external imbalance, the Government can operate only on internal conditions to correct it. The means by which the Government can influence these conditions, and the role of monetary policy in particular, are described in the earlier memorandum. To the extent that monetary policy is effective in influencing internal economic conditions, it will influence the balance of goods and services also.

28. These influences upon the balance of goods and services are very various in size and speed. A restriction of home demand will stimulate exports, but in most cases there will be a time lag, and this, in industries with a long period of production or lacking organised export outlets, may be long. It will also restrain imports. Similarly, a rise in interest rates may quickly induce some holders to reduce stocks, but the size of the reduction will depend upon expectations about prices and domestic trends generally. The order of magnitude of the probable effects of particular measures at particular times has to be assessed *ad hoc* in the light of the best appraisal than can be made of all the factors in the situation at home and abroad.

29. The *Property Income balance*, as Table I indicates, is normally in surplus because the United Kingdom on private account is a net creditor and has been adding regularly to its foreign investments, while Government debts, though large, carry low fixed interest charges. But the overall surplus on this account, is, in general, not at all closely connected with domestic conditions in its year to year variations. In the short run the annual return will mainly be determined by external conditions, and because events such as the Korean boom or the Abadan crisis can have large effects, the total can be volatile.

30. One important element is of course an exception in being closely tied to monetary policy; interest on overseas sterling holdings. This will vary with the volume held and the prevailing rates on the types of asset concerned. The cost of high interest

rates to the current balance can be quite an important factor, but it should be noted that, from the point of view of the short-term management of sterling:

(a) increases in this current outgoing can easily be out-weighed by gains (or prevention of losses) on capital account; and

(b) since most of the sterling held is on R.S.A. account, the payments tend in the short run to stay on deposit.

Table II sets out the main figures, so far as they can be estimated.

Monetary Policy and Long-term Investment

31. As was pointed out above, long-term investment in the N.S.A. is regulated through exchange control whilst that in the sterling area is not. United Kingdom private investment in the sterling area is however subject to much the same general influences and direct controls as similar investment in the United Kingdom itself. As is explained more fully in the earlier memorandum, private investment in the United Kingdom is influenced by action on the supply of funds for investment and by changing the climate for investment. Although of course the importance of the United Kingdom in international trade makes our balance of payments a significant factor in influencing conditions abroad, the climate for investment overseas is affected by many factors other than action by or conditions in the United Kingdom. But any restriction on the funds available for home investment will tend to exercise a curb on investment overseas. The limitations on the effectiveness of restraints on the supply of investment funds are discussed in the earlier memorandum, and these limitations—in particular the fact that investment financed from the retained profits of firms is only amenable to influence by monetary policy indirectly—are equally present in the external field. The demand of sterling area governments for long-term capital for new issues on the London market is in effect informally rationed in the process of normal market management and new issues by United Kingdom firms for overseas expenditure are subject to Capital Issues control. In as much as overseas borrowers have readier access to other capital markets, a tightening of conditions in the London capital market may

cause them to seek capital elsewhere. In such circumstances, the effect on overseas borrowing in London will be proportionately greater than on domestic borrowing. In general, monetary policy can be expected to have an effect on the level of United Kingdom investment overseas, though the presence of many other influences on such investment makes a quantitative assessment of the effect of monetary policy alone impossible.

32. The realisation of long-term financial assets in the United Kingdom by overseas holders, among whom of course the most important are R.S.A. countries, may be similarly influenced; a fall in capital values will for example discourage immediate disinvestment. But in general, such disinvestment will be mainly governed by the financial needs of the overseas holder. Monetary policy in this country does not necessarily have any direct or significant effect upon the plans an R.S.A. country may have to use some existing London funds to finance a long-term development programme.

Monetary Policy and Short-term Capital Movements

33. The transactions which are grouped under the heading of short-term capital movements belong, almost by definition, to the monetary field, and monetary policy must concern itself actively with them. In considering them it is useful to distinguish between 'normal' factors and 'confidence' factors. If only the former operated there would be no great problem, and short-term monetary policy would obey simple considerations of the supply and demand for short-term funds. An easing of the supply and the price of short-term sterling credit would tend to increase net lending (by encouraging the taking of credit and limiting the deposit of funds in London), and conversely for a tightening of credit conditions. In both cases there are potential effects on the reserves. Since the network of monetary centres round the world is technically a very perfect set of markets, policy would have to take careful account of overseas conditions, and it would be essential to keep short-term rates here in an appropriate relationship to those overseas.

34. If 'normal' factors were dominant, we would expect movements of short-term capital to be confined to two main kinds:

(*a*) those which merely arise as the financing transactions which offset the balance of current and long-term capital transactions; and

(*b*) those originating in changes in the relative credit conditions in different centres.

But 'confidence' factors (as well as variations in the barriers imposed by exchange control) have tended in most of the post-war period to dominate such 'normal' considerations. Changes in bank rate, etc., have been judged in the markets by their presumed effects upon questions of this kind rather than upon their immediate effects upon the credit situation. The central feature of 'confidence' has been that, having regard to the limitations of our external monetary position, doubt has existed over our capacity to carry out our domestic programmes without running into inflation. Other factors have from time to time had important effects but this has been the continuing one.

Reverse Effects

35. The preceding paragraphs have discussed the effects of monetary and general policy upon the balance of payments. But there are of course reverse effects; the balance of payments affects domestic monetary conditions (which will reflect back again upon the balance of payments). When, for example, the Exchange Equalisation Account is gaining gold or dollars, the need to finance the purchase adds to the total borrowing requirement of the Exchequer and this is liable to add to the total of bank deposits and also to banks' liquidity. Further, changes in overseas sterling holdings are likely to be accompanied by changes in direct overseas holdings of United Kingdom National Debt (Treasury Bills and Stock) and in money lent, for example, to the Discount Market. Such changes may absorb debt which would otherwise gravitate towards the banking system or may leave more debt to be held by the banking system. As an example of this, an increase in the external reserves which is accompanied by an increase in overseas sterling holdings may, at least in part, be the more easily financed by the Exchequer without recourse to the banking system, because overseas holders wish to raise their holdings of Treasury Bills or other

governmental indebtedness. As another illustration, if overseas sterling holdings are reduced, it is likely that 'outside' holdings of Treasury Bills (i.e. those outside the banks and the Discount Market's holdings with banks' call money) will fall and that bank holdings of Treasury Bills will rise in consequence. The exact sequences of events are very various and depend upon the nature of the holdings that change; they are likely to differ, for example, in respect of transactions with the R.S.A. and the N.S.A. The additional shifts of debt to or from the banking system, and additional Exchequer borrowing, due to changes in the external reserves and in overseas sterling holdings, form part of the general problem of monetary control.

Conclusions

36. The conclusions which can be drawn from this section of the paper are:

(*a*) *Exchange Control*

Within its limits, this is still strict and effective, but cannot prevent very large 'confidence' movements. Exchange control cannot therefore be regarded as a substitute for general economic policy; it can be no more than an adjunct.

(*b*) *Monetary Policy and Current Balance of Payments*

Two main elements are considered:

(i) *Goods and Services Balance*

Monetary policy can affect this *only* through its impact on the general internal economic conditions; to the extent that monetary policy is effective in influencing these conditions, it will influence the balance of goods and services also.

(ii) *Property Income*

In the short run the annual return will mainly be determined by external conditions, though in the long-term new capital investment overseas will have its effect upon income. The only important element in this balance which is directly affected by monetary policy is interest on overseas sterling holdings.

TABLE I

Analysis of Current Balance

£ million

	1946	1947	1948	1949	1950	1951	1952	1953	1954	1955	1956
Goods and services	—35	—373	—76	+29	+94	—473	+186	+39	+92	—134	+190
Property income (net)	44	114	187	162	337	217	93	163	225	160	178
Government balance:											
(*a*) Defence aid (net) and other special receipts (excluding offshore exports)	—	—	—	—	—	38	184	167	122	129	121
(*b*) Other Government (net)	—323	—149	—76	—139	—136	—171	—201	—177	—203	—217	—241
Migrants' funds, etc.	+16	—35	—34	—21	+5	—14	—15	—4	—8	—17	—15
Current balance	—298	—443	+1	+31	+300	—403	+247	+188	+228	—79	+233

TABLE II

Balance of Overseas Property Income

£ million

	1950	1951	1952	1953	1954	1955	1956
Payments on loans from foreign governments and debt to E.P.U.	—4	—43	—49	—51	—49	—45	—8
Receipts of loan interest	+28	+28	+28	+36	+36	+35	*
Interest on overseas sterling holdings (net)	—33	—42	—64	—71	—68	—97	—114
Other property income (net)	+346	+274	+178	+249	+306	+267	+300*
Total	+337	+217	+93	+163	+225	+160	+178

* 'Receipts of loan interest' are not yet separately available for 1956 and are included in 'Other property income (net)'.

(*c*) *Monetary Policy and Long-term Investment*

In general, monetary policy can be expected to have an effect on the level of United Kingdom investment overseas.

But monetary policy in this country does not necessarily have any direct or significant effect upon the plans an R.S.A. country may have to use existing London funds to finance a long-term development programme.

(*d*) *Monetary policy and Short-term Capital Movements*

It is necessary to distinguish between 'normal' and 'confidence' factors.

If *only* 'normal' factors operated, it would be necessary primarily to watch overseas conditions, and to keep short-term rates in appropriate relationship to those overseas.

But in fact in recent years 'confidence' factors have tended to dominate the 'normal'. The central feature of 'confidence' has been that, having regard to the limitations of our external monetary position, doubt has existed over our capacity to carry out our domestic programmes without running into inflation. Other factors have from time to time had important effects, but this has been the continuing one.

(*e*) *Reverse Effects*

These are the effects of the balance of payments on the internal monetary position. Changes in the external reserves alter the total of Government borrowing, and changes in sterling balances are likely to alter non-bank holdings of National Debt; these react upon the supply of money and upon bank liquidity. But these effects form part of the general problem of monetary control.

(ii) *Extracts from the Report of the Radcliffe Committee*
(Cmnd. 827)

Bank Rate and the Balance of Payments (Report, paragraphs 695–702)

695. The traditional weapon for protecting the reserves is the use of Bank Rate. The evidence submitted to us by the authori-

ties shows that there was anxiety about the state of the reserves at the time of every increase in bank rate since 1951 except that made in February 1956, and that the authorities believed that higher rates would have a demonstrable effect in reducing the pressure on sterling. On the other hand, we have had little evidence of actual movements of funds in response to changes in short-term rates, or of other measurable effects on the exchanges. The Bank of England has believed not that bank rate operates to make London a more attractive centre for the investment of funds but that, if altered at the right time and by the right amount, and if reinforced by other measures, it can serve to restore confidence in sterling, and reassure financial opinion abroad that the authorities will not remain quiescent in the face of inflationary dangers. It has not been put to us that an increase of bank rate, unaccompanied by Government statements and other measures, would accomplish a great deal if other factors were strongly inflationary. But the Bank of England does attribute some restraining influence to the use of bank rate in its own right; and the Governor claimed that on two occasions quite small movements had helped to prevent an overseas sterling crisis. We have discussed these arguments in Chapter VI (paragraphs 436–41), and so need not traverse them here.

696. While it is possible that bank rate has a stronger psychological effect abroad than at home, we take the view that this effect would only persist in either quarter if bank rate effectively influenced domestic demand or if it were taken to herald other measures in which resided the real power of restraint and which must eventually be seen to possess this power. The important issues are, therefore, what domestic effects follow changes in bank rate, and whether it is necessary or desirable to make use of bank rate rather than some other weapon in order to achieve them. Since we have already discussed in some detail in Chapter VI the impact of changes in bank rate on the domestic level of demand and activity, we need not pursue this particular type of effect, nor the assistance that it may lend to the balance of payments. We confine ourselves here to the direct effect of higher interest rates on capital movements.

697. The general tenor of the evidence sumbitted to us was

that in post-war conditions no large-scale transference of funds was to be expected in response to changes in short-term interest rates unsupported by other measures. Two important influences limiting this response have been fear of official interference with the movement of funds and fear of depreciation of sterling. If there is no confidence in the determination and power of the authorities to maintain the external value of sterling and freedom of convertibility on foreign account, a small interest differential is insufficient to attract funds to London and would not necessarily discourage borrowing in London. Such movement of funds as there has been has almost always, at least until lately, been covered in the forward exchange market; that is to say, the foreign holder of sterling has generally taken the precaution of selling it forward at a discount so as to avoid any larger loss through a possible devaluation of the pound. When the discount on forward sterling has been less than the interest differential he has still shown reluctance to move into sterling, because of fears that the forward contract might be overridden by further restrictions on the withdrawal of funds.

698. Although the Bank of England does not attribute a great deal of influence on movement of funds to changes in interest rates, it does appear to attach some importance to keeping London rates in line with rates in other centres and to assume that any prolonged or marked divergence would lead to a movement of funds either into or out of sterling. The most important occasion when this consideration seems to have been present to the minds of the authorities was at the time of the increase of bank rate to 4 per cent in March 1952, when many other central banks had been taking action to raise their rates from the rather low level at which they, in common with the Bank of England, had sustained them since the war. Another occasion when the Bank was influenced by the trend of rates in other centres was in May 1954, when bank rate was reduced to 3 per cent. On the movements which followed these changes the Governor of the Bank of England in his evidence commented:

'In all these cases there are two sides, a movement in of funds and a shifting out of borrowing. On the whole I would attach more importance to the latter than to the former. There have been occasions when our rates here have been lower than rates overseas, when there has been a lot of short-term semi-professional and commercial borrowing carried in this market which would more normally be carried, say, in Amsterdam or New York, and the raising of rates here has shifted that out.' (Qn. 1926)

699. The Bank subsequently gave us figures to illustrate the movements of funds that occurred before and after the increases in bank rate on the two occasions referred to above, but emphasised that it was difficult to isolate the effects of the change in interest rates from the simultaneous effects of other factors. These figures showed an increase in overseas borrowing from United Kingdom banks of about £25 million in the first two months of 1952, a fall of £60 million in the next four months, and a further fall of £55 million in the succeeding six months They also showed a rise in overseas borrowing beginning in the last quarter of 1953 (when market rates were already falling) and continuing throughout the spring and summer of 1954.

700. There is also some evidence that high rates (as opposed to an increase in rates) have tended to check borrowing in London. This is indeed the way in which bank rate used to work at a time when sterling credits played a much larger part in international finance than they do today. We were told that high London rates after September 1957 had attracted funds from overseas territories that had no exchange controls, and that some countries had introduced or intensified controls over banking and exchange in order to reduce or prevent the flow of funds to London. These effects, however, if confined to sterling countries, do nothing of themselves to strengthen the reserves and are merely offset by a corresponding rundown in overseas official holdings of sterling.

701. There have been some indications, particularly within the past year or so, that if high rates are not confined to the short-term market, but work their way through to long rates and to the yield on marketable securities, overseas investors may be induced to buy stocks and shares on the London market on a considerable scale. A movement of this kind may occur even when short-term funds do not move, since the holder of equities

may feel that he has already some hedge against a possible fall in the value of sterling.

702. The fact that changes in rates have had only a limited effect on the movements of funds in a period when sterling was weak does not imply that they will be correspondingly ineffective if sterling is strong. Once there is confidence in sterling, interest differentials tend to exert a more unobstructed influence on borrowing and lending, and the need to keep rates in line with those in other financial centres becomes more pressing. Thus the very change of circumstances that makes movements of interest rates more effective in defence of sterling make such movements less necessary.

Exchange Rates
(Report, paragraphs 708–18)

708. A second method of restoring equilibrium in the balance of payments is by depreciating the currency or allowing the rate of exchange to fluctuate freely. While we see no reason why the authorities should follow either of those courses in the foreseeable future, we think it right to examine the conditions under which one or other might become appropriate.

709. The pound has been allowed to fluctuate in value for two long spells during the present century, first between the suspension of the gold standard in 1914 and its restoration in 1925, and again between 1931 and 1939. Its exchange value against the dollar was roughly the same in 1939 as at the beginning of this century. It has since been twice devalued, first at the outbreak of war by 20 per cent and again in September 1949 by 30 per cent. There has therefore been some experience both of fluctuating rates and of devaluation to a new parity of exchange.

710. This experience has been sufficient to demonstrate both the inconvenience of a fluctuating pound and the impossibility of altering its value without regard to the interests of other countries which use sterling as an international currency. Either course of action intimately concerns the other members of the sterling area and would confront them with awkward dilemmas of policy. The preservation of a fixed rate of exchange undoubtedly offers the best prospect of avoiding strains and stresses

G

within the sterling area, except perhaps in highly abnormal conditions when the entire world economy is seriously out of balance and the area as a whole is under persistent pressure in its balance of payments with the non-sterling world.

711. Devaluation may take place as the only way out of an exchange crisis rather than as a deliberate decision of policy; but in that event it is likely to be due to earlier policy decisions or failure to take them in time. However it arises, it loses any advantages that it possesses the more often it happens. A fixed rate provides a firm basis on which to erect plans for trade and investment only if it can be confidently assumed that it will be maintained. A sequence of devaluations brings the worst of both worlds: on the one hand it introduces uncertainty, and gives speculators a strong incentive to anticipate the next adjustment in rates without running any real risk; on the other hand it withholds the flexibility that might be afforded by a fluctuating rate, with its power to yield more gradually to market forces.

712. There appear to us to be three sets of conditions in which a change in parity merits consideration. The first two involve a divergence between the trend of costs and prices in the United Kingdom and in other countries; the third arises when the balance of payments remains in chronic deficit without any marked change in relative costs and prices.

713. A divergence between United Kingdom and overseas costs and prices may take two forms: either in the terms on which the United Kingdom exchanges exports for imports or in the terms on which United Kingdom manufacturers compete with overseas manufacturers. A large change in the terms of trade is usually concentrated on United Kingdom import prices rather than on export prices, which are relatively sluggish. Because of the importance of imports in the economy of the United Kingdom, a rise in import prices affects not only the balance of payments but also the level of domestic costs, either directly through raw material prices or indirectly through the cost of living and the movement of wage and other costs. Appreciation of the pound would help to steady import prices if they were increasing in terms of foreign currencies, and so would check the spread of inflation to the economy of the

United Kingdom. But it might at the same time put a brake on
United Kingdom exports if it obliged exporters to accept lower
sterling prices, and it might also create some distrust in sterling
among holders who found difficulty in reconciling an appreciation of the currency with a deterioration in the balance of
payments.

714. Altering the rate of exchange is thus an uncertain
method of warding off the inflationary effects of a rise in import
prices, and its use for this purpose could only be contemplated
if the rise were a particularly violent one. Moreover, since a
large proportion of imports into the United Kingdom are
drawn from countries that would be likely to appreciate their
currencies simultaneously with the United Kingdom, revalua-
tion of the pound would not necessarily achieve its object of
stabilising sterling prices but might merely serve to raise the
price of the United Kingdom's staple imports in terms of gold or
dollars.

715. The situation is quite different when there is a progressive deterioration in the competitive position of United Kingdom
exports on world markets. In such a situation the relevant consideration is the movement in the price of United Kingdom
exports, mainly manufactures, compared with the price of
similar goods manufactured elsewhere. Devaluation, which
might seem capable of restoring the position, could accomplish
little in the short run because it takes a good deal of time and
considerable outlay in selling costs for most types of manufactures to win their way in export markets, especially those
markets in which sales effort has not previously been concentrated. But if the competitive handicap has been persistent and
the devaluation more than removes it, the price advantage that
results should not only bring to an end the gradual loss of
markets but should eventually reverse the process.

716. This does not mean that the United Kingdom should
be easily moved to devalue sterling when costs have been increasing faster in this country than abroad. On the contrary,
everything possible should be done to bring the rise in domestic
costs and prices under control and to put an end to the strain on
the reserves by lagging behind the movement abroad instead of

outstripping it. But experience has revealed no other instrument as powerful as devaluation that can be used to restore competitive power; in conditions in which the failure of exports to make headway is plainly restricting the level of domestic activity and other countries are not experiencing similar difficulties, it offers a way of escape that cannot be excluded.

717. The third situation is in a sense a variant of this. Competitive power must be measured, not against some previous level of comparative costs, but in relation to the structural adjustments in exports and imports that have to be accomplished. If exports are insufficient to yield a satisfactory balance of payments, or if overseas demand falls off for the range of goods in which the British export trades specialise, it may be necessary to accept a lower price in order to secure the necessary increase in earnings. Any attempt on the United Kingdom's part to obtain a larger share of world trade in manufactures must involve the offer either of a more attractive range of exports (which is no doubt preferable but depends upon the unforeseeable course taken by world demand) or of the traditional range of exports on more attractive terms. Devaluation can make the terms on which British goods are offered more attractive, and, if the response of foreign customers is elastic, will add to export earnings. Thus it is a measure which may have to be taken if long-term changes in the structure of world markets or in the relationship between the components of the United Kingdom's balance of payments are throwing the economy progressively out of external balance.

718. These are all situations with which experience since the war has made us familiar. They may occur again, and other methods of dealing with them may prove ineffective. Only then would it be right to consider changing the external value of the currency: not as a normal instrument of monetary policy, but as a measure capable, in default of acceptable alternatives, of bringing about some enduring adjustment in the country's economic structure, correcting some long-standing lack of balance in its competitive position, or checking any violent inflationary or deflationary pressure that may reach it from abroad.

Overseas Investment
(Report, paragraphs 731–43)

731. We now consider the special problems of long-term investment. London is by tradition one of the great capital markets of the world, and one which has been over the past century the first recourse of many of the less developed countries. The overseas investments built up by the United Kingdom, mainly outside Europe, have contributed to the cheapening of transport costs, the enlargement of the world market, and the advancement of living standards through new trading opportunities. Apart from the private return to the investor, they have formed an important element in the balancing of the United Kingdom's international accounts and of the financial resources that could be mobilised in time of war. They are also an integral part of the system that binds together in mutual dependence the economies of the United Kingdom and the great primary producing countries of the world.

732. Control over the export of capital was almost unthinkable when the pound was strong and British savings were more than sufficient to meet domestic requirements. It was introduced in the 1930s in the shape of a Foreign Transactions Advisory Committee, to which proposed issues on foreign account were referred for advice; this was the body which later became the Capital Issues Committee. At that stage the intention was to strengthen sterling by limiting transfers across the exchanges. Since the war this aim has been combined with that of relieving pressure on the total resources of the United Kingdom and maintaining a balance between the need for additional capital at home and overseas. This is a much more restrictive objective than the first, since there are many types of loan that would do little or nothing to weaken the pound but might aggravate the shortage of capital in this country.

733. The desire to strengthen sterling explains why control is stricter over investment outside the sterling area than within it. A resident of the United Kingdom is free to move his own funds to any part of the sterling area, but becomes subject to exchange control immediately he seeks to transfer capital to a non-sterling

country. Any such transfer involving, say, a direct business investment in a Canadian subsidiary, requires specific sanction on its merits. No such sanction is needed in the case of a similar investment within the sterling area. Where a public issue has to be made capital issues consent is required, and this consent has hardly ever been given to an issue by a non-sterling borrower. Capital issues consent for issues by sterling borrowers outside the United Kingdom has been confined to Commonwealth governments; with only one exception, no subordinate authority in the rest of the sterling area has been allowed to raise money by issues on the London market. Commonwealth governments wishing to raise capital on the London market must first satisfy the United Kingdom Treasury that the loan is necessary in order to support a well-conceived programme of development, and have later to agree with the Bank of England on the timing of the issue and the capacity of the market to absorb it. They may be encouraged by the Treasury to borrow in some other market or may themselves elect to do so.

734. We inquired whether this 'informal rationing in the process of normal market management' by the Treasury and the Bank was likely to be a continuing feature, or whether it was envisaged that Commonwealth governments would ultimately be free to go on the London market as and when they wished. The Treasury took the view that, unless rates of interest rose very high, which they thought would have undesirable consequences, the capital shortage made it likely that the existing arrangements would last for as far ahead as it was possible to see. While we do not dissent from this view, we think it important that overseas investment should not be looked upon as a mere residual, to be adjusted by restrictions on new issues to the balance of other items in the international accounts of the United Kingdom. It is no doubt inevitable that the central governments of Commonwealth countries should be given priority of access to the London market over their subordinate authorities; but the role of these authorities is likely to be an expanding one, so that it would be most unwise to exclude them indefinitely from the opportunity of borrowing in London. It is also highly desirable that there should be a sufficient margin in the balance of payments to

allow of a gradual increase in the credit extended to overseas
purchasers of British goods. Various forms of direct investment
abroad could with advantage be increased if the existing controls were relaxed. For these reasons we were glad to learn from
the Treasury that their calculations are now based on the
assumption of a larger current account surplus in the early
1960s, sufficient to leave room for a substantial increase in
Government lending and private overseas investment. In assuming that the 'desirable' balance of payments surplus should
average £450 million a year, the Treasury allows £150 million
for repaying short-term liabilities and building up reserves, £90
million for new governmental lending and repayments of loans,
and the remainder, a little over £200 million, for net additions
to private overseas investments. While these calculations do not
allow for any change of policy, a current surplus of £450 million
a year might in practice permit of some liberalisation, particularly of investment within the Commonwealth.

735. It would be a mistake to suppose that existing restrictions have reduced overseas investment to negligible proportions.
There are restrictions on new issues, foreign exchange is not as a
general rule made available for portfolio investment in non-
sterling area securities, and there is an exchange control over
direct investment outside the sterling area. But one of the most
important forms of investment, the use of retained earnings to
maintain or develop overseas assets, escapes control altogether
if it is within the sterling area, and is usually permitted in non-
sterling countries. It has been estimated that reinvestment by
United Kingdom firms out of overseas earnings is of the order of
£200 million a year, and this is not far short of the rate of net
overseas investment in recent years.

736. We have been provided by the Bank of England with
tentative estimates of the scale of United Kingdom investment
overseas since 1945.

737. The figures in Table 33 are gross, and so take no account
of loans to the United Kingdom Government, investments by
non-residents in the United Kingdom, repayments of capital,
realisation of United Kingdom debts abroad, and so on. Some
of these items are large, even in comparison with the totals in

TABLE 33

United Kingdom gross external investment, 1946–57
£ million

	1946–51	1952	1953	1954	1955	1956	1957	1946–57
Private Investment[1]								
Sterling Area	910	160	200	210	170	210	250	2,110
Rest of World	380	80	70	110	140	210	140	1,130
Public Investment								
Sterling Area	86	12	17	26	25	19	22	207
Rest of World	259	11	7	—	19	2	8	306
Total	1,635	263	294	346	354	441	420	3,753

[1] These estimates are extremely uncertain, especially those for the sterling area. Investment from retained profits is only partly covered, and the resulting figures are known to be seriously incomplete.

Table 33: for example, while the United Kingdom Government and official agencies lent just over £500 million during the twelve years covered by Table 33, the Government repaid £750 million to foreign governments, was itself repaid £470 million borrowed £1,700 million and subscribed £565 million to international organisations. Net external investment, public and private, may have totalled about £1,300 million, nearly all of it in the second half of the twelve year period.

738. The main element in the total has undoubtedly been private investment. The gross figures suggest a steady rise over the past five or six years from about £250 million to roughly £400 million per annum, with an increasing proportion going outside the sterling area. A large part of private investment abroad is in the oil industry, which also accounts for most of the sharp increase in the past few years. The official estimates of net long-term capital movements show a less distinct upward trend, and average only £200 million over the past five or six years. The difference between this and the gross figure is presumably due to repayments, realisation of assets, and investment by non-

residents in the United Kingdom. Nearly the whole of the net movement is to sterling area countries, whereas the gross figures show a large outflow to non-sterling countries.

739. The magnitude of United Kingdom investment overseas led some of our witnesses to suggest that, so far from removing any restrictions on it, the Government should try to limit it still further. They argued that it was competitive on the one hand with domestic investment, which was inadequate, and on the other with the rebuilding of reserves to a more desirable level. In their view the United Kingdom has been trying to add too rapidly to her long-term overseas assets and it would have been preferable to use a larger part of the current surplus to add to the gold and foreign exchange reserves or to pay off short-term liabilities. The example of Germany is in point: with a favourable balance about twice as large as Britain's, Germany has invested very little abroad on private account and not a great deal on public account, so that a large part of her substantial surplus has been available to swell the reserves or to finance short-term credits to other countries.

740. If it were possible to choose freely between an addition of £500 million to the reserves over the next few years and an equivalent addition to long-term investments abroad, few people would be likely to hesitate long over the choice. The sacrifice of income involved in purchasing gold and foreign exchange in preference to long-term securities would not be too high a price to pay for greater immunity from sudden crises in the exchanges. Equally it would be foolish to export capital from the United Kingdom if that meant denuding British industry and thus impairing its competitive power. But on three grounds the choice is not a free one.

741. First, as we emphasised in Chapter II, it is one of the objectives of the United Kingdom Government's policy to contribute to the more rapid development of Commonwealth countries. This being so, it cannot discourage the investment which has contributed so notably to past development, nor stand in the way of loans to members of the Commonwealth, especially if there is no other market in which they can borrow on reasonable terms. It must be prepared, therefore, to main-

tain a balance of payments sufficiently favourable to leave a margin for loans and other investments. This margin must be correspondingly widened to allow of grants in aid of colonial development.

742. Secondly, even from the standpoint of self-interest investment in overseas countries is urgent and valuable. Most of it is in countries that are at once important suppliers of the United Kingdom and large purchasers of United Kingdom goods. Investment in those countries contributes to an expansion or cheapening in the supplies of goods which the United Kingdom imports and generates additional export opportunities. Those among them that are members of the sterling area also look to the United Kingdom, as banker for the area, to provide capital to meet their reasonable requirements. If the capital is not provided in the form of outright loans, as was usual in the nineteenth century, then they expect that it should be provided as export credits by the United Kingdom when supplying industrial equipment.

743. Finally, the fact that it might be preferable to have less investment in long-term assets and a faster build-up of the reserves does not mean that the Government need only tighten its control over capital exports to make the reserves increase. The variables that go to make up the balance of payments react on one another in so many different ways that it is very hard to predict how a change in the total balance would be divided between the constituent elements. Action to limit investment abroad might at first reinforce the reserves, or more probably, in view of the high proportion of such investment in the sterling area, reduce sterling liabilities. But the restriction of one of their sources of foreign capital would be bound to reduce the imports of the borrowing countries, and some part of this reduction would fall on United Kingdom exports. No doubt this would afford an opportunity of diverting supplies to other markets or of re-deploying resources in the United Kingdom so as to make a smaller call on imports. But there might also be some fall in the level of economic activity, or the capital previously invested abroad might be diverted to home uses. No one could foretell in advance the precise outcome of the initial restriction on the

export of capital; and there would certainly be no automatic gain to the reserves equal to the fall in overseas investment.

(iii) *The Impact on the Overseas Sterling Area*

(Extracts from Memoranda submitted to the Radcliffe Committee by the Central Banks of certain sterling countries. Source: *Principal Memoranda of Evidence*, Vol. 1)

COMMONWEALTH BANK OF AUSTRALIA

65. The sterling area can be said to comprehend in a broad sense a general complex of monetary arrangements. In this broad sense they would include:

(*a*) The use of sterling to finance external trade and payments.

(*b*) Facilities for holding reserves in sterling.

(*c*) Arrangements for trade restrictions; and

(*d*) Other financial relationships.

66. The sterling area is a voluntary association of nations which is not subject to formal rules and obligations. While its arrangements are the product of a long historical development, they are still based on considerations of mutual interest. The United Kingdom is an important market for the export products of members of the sterling area, the sterling bill is a predominant instrument of international trade, London provides an efficient money market and remains a source of investment capital, and there are considerable advantages in maintaining central reserves and a dollar pool. The importance of these advantages, of course, has varied according to the conditions prevailing from time to time, and it may be useful to look at the whole question from an Australian point of view under the headings outlined above.

(*a*) *The Use of Sterling to Finance External Trade and Payments*

67. Because so much of Australia's export and import trade takes place with the United Kingdom and other countries prepared to accept and make payments in sterling, it is convenient for Australia to finance external trade transactions in sterling.

For this purpose the sterling area arrangements are well developed and are technically efficient. But it is to be noted, nevertheless, that high interest rates in London with their consequential effect on the terms on which sterling bills are negotiated abroad as well as any tightening of the credit facilities available in London for world trade can have unfavourable effects on Australian exports.

68. The pattern of Australia's trade is essentially multilateral. Transactions between Australia and non-sterling countries outside the dollar area show a substantial surplus which is normally used to finance trade deficits with the sterling area and the dollar area. Our trade with the dollar area forms only a relatively small part, some 10–15 per cent, of our total trade. Broadly speaking we draw on the sterling area dollar pool to finance our deficit with this area. However, our surplus position with other non-dollar, non-sterling countries, more particularly those European countries covered by E.P.U. arrangements, adds to the gold and dollar receipts of the United Kingdom. The sterling area gold and dollar reserve arrangements enable us to finance our trade with the dollar area smoothly and efficiently.

69. Since 1931 the Australian currency has maintained a stable parity with the £ sterling of £A125=£E100. The rates for other currencies quoted by Australian banks are based on this rate and the rate in the London market for the currency concerned. The major Australian trading banks have branches in London and the London money market has always been an important source of finance for overseas importers of Australian products. Exchange dealings in foreign currencies are generally arranged in London through the banks' London offices, to whom the wide facilities of the London foreign exchange market are available.

(b) *Facilities for Holding Reserves in Sterling*

70. It is essential for any trading country to hold its international reserves in a fairly liquid and convenient form. In the case of Australia, over 50 per cent of our total exports and imports take place with members of the sterling area. In addition,

a further 30–40 per cent of our trade is with the non-dollar group of countries and nearly all of this trade is with O.E.E.C. countries and members of the E.P.U., or with countries holding reserves, and accepting payments, in sterling. It is clear, then, that almost 90 per cent of our total trade can be financed in sterling and we have, therefore, usually kept large liquid reserves in that currency.

71. In general, this arrangement has been convenient from our point of view. Close co-operation with the Bank of England, and the facilities which are offered by the London money market, enable us to invest our reserves in a way which ensures flexibility and reasonable returns. There are advantages, however, in spreading our reserves over different forms of holdings. Since Australia is a gold producing country, it is natural enough that she should hold some gold reserves. While these may be regarded as separate reserves, in one sense, they have been used on occasions to reinforce the sterling area central reserves, e.g. the sale to the United Kingdom of £25 million in September 1956. It has been found convenient, also, to build up small holdings of dollars as Australian capital liabilities in terms of dollars have risen. These have been small in relation to the sterling component of our reserves but they have, we believe, materially strengthened Australia's status as a borrower in the international market.

72. One point which should perhaps be mentioned in this respect is that the real purchasing power of the reserves which we hold in sterling is determined by the amount of foreign goods which these reserves will purchase at any point of time, not only in the United Kingdom but also in the other countries with which we trade. It is a question both of the movement in sterling prices and also of the relationships which are maintained between the £ sterling and other currencies. Any movement in sterling prices may affect also the prices of Australian exports, and change the terms of trade, either to our advantage or disadvantage. Nevertheless it is clear that if sterling prices continue to rise, especially if they rise relatively to currencies which would provide a practical alternative for our holdings of reserves, then Australia must suffer a real capital loss.

(c) Arrangements for Trade Restrictions

73. The sterling area has provided a framework within which a larger and smoother flow of trade can develop. However, it has been necessary from time to time for members of the sterling area to take measures which would ensure that their drawings on the sterling area gold and dollar reserves were kept to reasonable proportions. This has meant in particular the imposition of discriminatory trade restrictions and an agreement to pursue domestic policies consistent with sterling area objectives.

74. From some points of view discrimination has been of value, not only to the sterling area as a whole, but also to individual countries. These restrictions have, however, had considerable disadvantages and have deprived sterling area countries of access to cheaper sources of supply for particular import items. They have been regarded as essentially a temporary device and sterling area policy, since 1952, has been directed towards the reduction and ultimate elimination of this dollar discrimination.

75. While the sterling area gold and dollar reserves are considered inadequate, further moves to the full convertibility of sterling will no doubt be inhibited. In these circumstances, it will be difficult, from time to time, to avoid applying some form of discriminatory trade and payments restrictions. The problem, however, is not merely one of increasing the size of the sterling area reserves. In the final analysis it will depend rather on the capacity of the sterling area as a whole to achieve and maintain a sufficiently strong balance of payments position with the rest of the world. The long-term objective should be to achieve an internal situation where the relationship between currencies would not need to be supported by restrictions on current payments. However, since restrictions may be needed from time to time to protect the sterling area reserves, it would be unwise to completely dismantle exchange control machinery, even when greater progress towards convertibility becomes practicable.

(d) Other Financial Relationships

76. Australia is a rapidly developing country which requires substantial amounts of investment capital to carry through its

development programmes. It is not possible for us to provide the total savings required from our own resources and therefore we have been heavily dependent on overseas capital. A large proportion of overseas capital has come in the past from the United Kingdom in particular, and this flow, in recent years, has been maintained at a reasonably high rate and has been facilitated by our continuing membership of the sterling area. However, for some years capital has been virtually unobtainable from the United Kingdom on official account and Australia has, therefore, been obliged to extend its official borrowing to other financial centres. We have also received considerable private capital from the dollar area and, in addition, have arranged a number of loans from the I.B.R.D. and from the American market and banking institutions, in addition to smaller loans from Canada and Switzerland.

Reserve Bank of New Zealand

96. For New Zealand the sterling exchange standard evolved during the nineteenth century as a natural outcome of personal, political, commercial and financial ties with the United Kingdom. There was no alternative to a procedure whereby New Zealand traded mainly with the United Kingdom and other Commonwealth countries, financed virtually all its foreign exchange transactions in sterling, held sterling as its principal external reserve (apart from some gold) and maintained its exchange rate at a fixed rate with sterling. No alternative has ever been seriously considered.

97. This position has not been basically altered by the adoption of formal sterling area arrangements in 1939 and their continuation, with modifications, ever since. Conformity with centralised rules of exchange control has been readily accepted, especially in wartime of course, and the progressive relaxation of the discriminatory elements in exchange control has been welcomed. It remains true, however, that there has been no attempt made in New Zealand to weigh up the relative weight of the advantages and disadvantages of belonging to the sterling area. When sterling is strong and convertible, no problem arises.

When sterling is thoroughly inconvertible, the reasons are clear and inescapable. In between those two extremes there is the belief that New Zealand's membership of the sterling system is inevitable and the hope that discriminatory restrictions on payments to the non-sterling area are perhaps only temporary.

98. There are a few aspects of the present situation which call for comment.

(1) New Zealand is in most years a net contributor to the central gold and dollar reserves of the sterling area, if account is taken of the large surplus earned with O.E.E.C. countries, 75 per cent of which is now being settled in gold. This surplus is due mainly to sales of wool to European countries, and is large enough to more than offset the deficit usually incurred in direct transactions with the dollar area.

(2) There can be circumstances in which monetary action, taken by the United Kingdom authorities to meet a situation arising out of United Kingdom responsibilities as an international banker, may have unsettling and perhaps harmful repercussions on New Zealand. The 7 per cent bank rate of last September is a case in point. It affected New Zealand in the following ways:

(a) It probably accentuated the fall in commodity prices, notably wool, and thus contributed towards New Zealand's present balance of payments difficulties.

(b) When, as a result of those difficulties, New Zealand borrowed in London in April 1958, the terms were not favourable compared with those of earlier loans or with those of other markets.

(c) The abnormal disparity between bank overdraft rates in United Kingdom and New Zealand was the reason why some firms (mainly engaged in trade in meat and wool) shifted their borrowing from London to New Zealand, thereby causing a delay in export receipts and an outflow of short-term capital. These changes came at a time when we could ill afford them.

(3) At times it would have been helpful to have an arrangement whereby a sterling area country in balance of payments difficulties could obtain short-term credits from other

countries in the area. In this way it would be easier to maintain a high level of trade and stability of prices. Such an
arrangement would be specially helpful to New Zealand,
whose external trade per head is very high but subject to
marked fluctuations. We have no specific proposal to put
forward, but recommend further study of this topic.

(4) The administrative arrangements concerning sterling area
exchange control are quite satisfactory. The Reserve Bank
is in frequent contact with the Bank of England by cable,
by correspondence, and by personal visits, in addition to
routine daily arrangements. There is no lack of opportunity
for consultation on technical matters.

(5) At the policy level consultation takes place among most
sterling countries through the Commonwealth Liaison
Committee, or at Finance Ministers' meetings associated
with the Annual Meetings of the International Monetary
Fund and the International Bank. The Reserve Bank does
not participate in these meetings, though it was represented
at some of the earlier special Conferences of Commonwealth
Finance Ministers. There are times when it seems desirable
that consultation on policy should be more regular and
thorough, but we recognise the difficulties and have no
specific recommendation to make.

South African Reserve Bank

60. Arrangements with the Bank of England for the conduct
of the Reserve Bank's sterling account, including the investment
of funds, the custody and the sale of gold are eminently satisfactory.

61. There is, moreover, close co-operation with the Bank of
England in the exchange of statistical information and colla-
boration in the application of exchange control procedures,
particularly in respect of South African imports from, and exports to, non-sterling countries which are financed through
sterling.

62. In this latter respect, however, there is evidence that the
'credit squeeze' and the high level of interest rates in the United

H

Kingdom have resulted in some switch of such financing from the United Kingdom to the Union, with unfavourable repercussions on the Union's balance of payments. This has also applied to the financing of trade between the Union and the sterling area.

63. The same measures in the United Kingdom have likewise adversely affected the Union's balance of payments by causing certain United Kingdom parent companies to draw the maximum possible amount of funds from their local subsidiaries, not only in respect of available cash reserves and undistributed profits, but also such further funds as the subsidiaries have been able to raise by local borrowing. In addition, there was a substantial dis-investment from the United Kingdom during 1957 —the net outflow of capital on private account (including financing transactions mentioned above) being estimated at approximately £28 million.

64. Various reasons have been advanced for the waning popularity of South African gold mining securities in the United Kingdom and on the Continent, but one factor which is of significance is seldom mentioned. In the original concept of the sterling area as a closed area, ringed by uniform exchange controls on the movement of capital to non-sterling countries, but within which there was free movement of funds, the under-developed members of the area relied on the United Kingdom as their principal source of capital for development, and the exchange controls, by drastically curtailing non-sterling investment, ensured that investment funds seeking an outlet from the United Kingdom were channelled into sterling area investments.

65. During recent years, however, relaxations by the United Kingdom exchange control on non-sterling capital investment, particularly in Canada, have had the effect of reducing the volume of sterling funds which would otherwise have been available for investment in the sterling area, and there is, moreover, evidence in the Union that at least part of United Kingdom dis-investment here has resulted from the switching by United Kingdom investors into Canadian (hard currency) investments. In other words, South African gold shares have, as a result of United Kingdom exchange control relaxations,

suffered a loss of attractiveness as a hedge against a possible sterling devaluation.

66. Furthermore, the control of capital issues in the United Kingdom, although basically an internal measure, has wider repercussions on other sterling area countries—a recent case in point has been the limitation of a proposed issue to existing United Kingdom shareholders of convertible notes by the Rhodesian Anglo-American Corporation, which resulted in the Anglo-American Corporation of South Africa, who had under-written the issue, being compelled to finance the Rhodesian company to the extent of the difference from its own, and there-fore from South African, resources.

67. Also, primarily on domestic considerations, other indirect obstacles have been placed in the United Kingdom on the free outward movement of funds to other sterling countries, and while it is difficult to assess the cumulative effect of these measures, it is known that restrictions imposed by the Revenue Authorities on the transfer of domicile from the United King-dom to the Union of mining houses and other holding com-panies, whose assets are primarily held in South Africa, have adversely affected the Union.

68. The combination of these various factors, many of which were admittedly designed as internal measures for the protection of sterling and the United Kingdom balance of payments, has affected not only the Union, but other sterling area countries who have been compelled, in varying degree, to move away from the original concept of the sterling area and, in an en-deavour to protect their own position, to impose restrictions on the free movement of funds to other members of the sterling area.

69. The Union always attached great importance to the free movement of funds within the sterling area and regarded it as an essential feature of the area system, not only because it facilitated the natural net outflow of investment funds from the mature economy of the United Kingdom to the young and developing countries of the area, but also because it was inti-mately associated with the United Kingdom's function as banker to the area. In the past, therefore, the Union was able to

rely upon a varying but reasonable net inflow of funds from the United Kingdom, but, as mentioned previously, the picture has recently changed and the Union has experienced a significant net outflow of funds in various forms to the United Kingdom, which has seriously affected the Union's balance of payments, particularly as, since the middle of 1957, it happened to coincide with a substantial increase in imports and an appreciable decrease in the exports of various farm and mineral products.

70. The Union reluctantly imposed its first restrictions on exchange transactions with the sterling area as a protective measure in February, 1956, when the Bank of England rate was raised from $4\frac{1}{2}$ to $5\frac{1}{2}$ per cent, while the Union preferred to avoid a further general increase in its rate structure. The restrictions, however, were applied only to Union residents and were administered very liberally; they were withdrawn in February 1957, when the Bank of England lowered its rate to 5 per cent but were re-imposed in September 1957 when the Bank of England rate was raised to 7 per cent. They were again administered very liberally until the 8 May 1958, when it was announced that, owing to the persistent decline in the Union's reserves, stricter controls were henceforth to be applied to exchange transactions by Union residents with sterling area countries, as in the case of non-sterling countries. It was, however, decided to continue a liberal attitude towards the Federation of Rhodesia and Nyasaland, as the withdrawal of the previous individual exemption limit of £10,000 could, if strictly applied, be embarrassing to the Federation which is also experiencing serious balance of payments difficulties, mainly due to factors outside its control.

71. From the foregoing it will be apparent that, if the sterling area is to survive as a partnership for the benefit of all members of that partnership, more consideration must be given by each of the partners to the effect of his individual actions, both internal and external, on the financial and economic well-being of his other partners. This applies more particularly to the United Kingdom which, as the hub of the sterling area, has a correspondingly greater influence on the smaller outer members of the area than they can possibly have on the hub or even on one another.

72. The drastic measures which have been taken by the United Kingdom have undoubtedly tended to impose an excessive strain upon the Union and other countries of the area. The circumstances and aims of these countries often differ materially from those of the United Kingdom and, for that reason chiefly, they are frequently unable to apply measures of similar severity without serious danger to the future development of their economies, so that a resort to restrictive devices alien to the spirit of the area arrangements becomes practically unavoidable. Moreover, while past experience suggests that the phase of severe monetary controls in the United Kingdom may be expected to give way in due course to a milder regime, it does not support the belief that the stringency will not return when seasonal or other factors again become adverse.

73. From the United Kingdom's point of view, it is apparent that the measures adopted have been of material assistance in overcoming the country's immediate difficulties and, in conjunction with the willingness of the authorities to take them, have bolstered confidence in sterling in the short run. On the other hand, it seems equally apparent that the frequent need to resort to what are virtually crisis measures, even in moderately adverse circumstances, tends to undermine longer-term confidence in sterling.

74. Whatever the specific circumstances that have prompted the repeated resort to measures of this nature—and the character of the measures is an important factor in the situation—there is no doubt that their severity has been largely dictated by the precariously low level of the United Kingdom's reserves relative to the potential claims on them, that is, by a lack of the necessary degree of liquidity. The average level of liquidity in the United Kingdom since the war, in other words, has left little or no leeway for meeting adverse developments by that moderate use of the available monetary instruments which would be consistent with the status of sterling as an international currency and the United Kingdom's position as banker to the sterling area.

75. The means by which liquidity in the United Kingdom— and in most other countries of the world where it is also at a very

low level—may be increased effectively and speedily and on a reasonably permanent basis, therefore, is a matter of prime concern. In this respect, it is clear that there is little prospect of improving liquidity to the necessary extent by reducing the potential claims on the reserves, as this would obviously involve an excessive and damaging degree of deflation. The only practicable solution, therefore, lies in securing a suitable increase in reserves.

76. It has been suggested in this connection, for example, that the United States should extend a large stabilisation loan to the United Kingdom or, alternatively, that the resources of the International Monetary Fund should be increased by a substantial addition of gold and/or dollars. The merit of these and similar proposals, however, lies chiefly in the assistance they can provide when liquidity crises have developed and not in their contribution to an effective and reasonably permanent solution to the world-wide liquidity problem. They would not, for example, increase global liquidity, and they rest on the assumption, therefore, that liquidity in the creditor countries, particularly the United States, is so much more than adequate for their own needs that they can afford to underwrite, adequately and on a lasting basis, liquidity in the rest of the world. This assumption, however, is difficult to sustain, for American reserves at the end of 1957 amounted to 15 per cent of the money supply plus short-term foreign liabilities, while the latter were almost equal to free reserves in the United States, that is, reserves in excess of the statutory minimum. The United States, in short, also appears to have relatively little room for manoeuvre for a country with its international responsibilities, and would face a difficult situation if confidence in the dollar should decline for any reason.

77. Furthermore, borrowed reserves carry an interest burden and have to be repaid. If they actually have to be used in meeting a crisis—and normally they are only likely to become available when a crisis threatens or has actually developed and confidence has already suffered a set-back—there is no guarantee that repayment can be effected without undue strain, or that it will not depend upon the maintenance of stringent controls. These considerations are particularly relevant in the case of the

short-term assistance which the Fund can render, and would also apply, in large part, to the suggestion that gold reserves might be centralised in the Fund, even if countries could be persuaded to agree to this course.

78. While such proposals, thus, are to be welcomed as a supplementary source of strength when circumstances become critical, they are not the answer to the problem of securing an effective and lasting increase in liquidity which is so essential a factor in preventing the development of serious crises. This depends chiefly upon the existence of a level of owned reserves which, in relation to the claims on them, is sufficient to maintain confidence in the national currency at home and abroad under such adverse conditions as can reasonably be expected to arise, and without reliance—particularly in the leading countries—upon the maintenance or repeated use of excessively severe monetary and other controls.

79. In the light of the foregoing, the only practicable and lasting solution to the liquidity problem, and one from which the United Kingdom and the Commonwealth in particular would benefit, would appear to lie in a substantial increase in the monetary value of the world's gold reserves which, in turn, can only be achieved through an appropriate increase in the price of gold in terms of all national currencies. Admittedly, there is opposition to this move, particularly in the United States, which rests chiefly upon what appear to be rather exaggerated fears of possible inflationary consequences and benefits to the Russian area. But considerable opposition is also likely to be encountered in giving effect to the other proposals mentioned earlier, and in these circumstances it would seem both reasonable and desirable to concentrate upon that proposal which is likely to provide the most satisfactory long-term solution of the liquidity problem.

BANK OF RHODESIA AND NYASALAND

27. From the point of view of this Bank, the present sterling area arrangements are, in general, very satisfactory. The main advantages to us of the present system lie in the following:

   (i) The London money market provides the best available outlet for the investment of the Federation's external reserves;

  (ii) The London capital market is the principal source of the Federation's long-term external borrowing;

 (iii) The sterling system provides the machinery for the multilateral clearing of our foreign payments;

 (iv) The intimate relationships which exist between the Bank of England and the Bank of Rhodesia and Nyasaland are of inestimable practical value.

28. With regard to (i) above, it should be made clear that this Bank as custodian of the country's main external assets has an overriding interest in seeing that its investments are safely employed. It follows that the maintenance by sterling of its internal and external value, both in the short and long term, is of prime concern to us. We welcome, therefore, the many assurances that have, from time to time, been given by the United Kingdom Government that no change in the external value of sterling is contemplated. I should point out that since the value of our currency unit has been defined (*vide* Federal Government Notice No. 52 of 1956) as equal to one pound sterling, any change in the external value of sterling would immediately raise a difficult question of policy for the Federation. I should point out, however, that the Governor-General is fully empowered to determine the value of the Rhodesian pound.

29. We heartily endorse also the measures which have in recent months been taken to stabilise the internal value of sterling, since it is of considerable importance to us that the purchasing power of our reserves held in London should not be eroded by currency depreciation. In this connection, however, while we strongly approve the motives which led to the raising last year of the bank rate in London to an exceptionally high level, the existence of a high interest rate structure in London has tended to accentuate our own balance of payments problem. Capital which might otherwise have come to the Federation has been induced by the high returns available there to stay in London. We have seen several cases of parent companies located in the United Kingdom instructing their subsidiaries to

draw on unused lines of credit at local banks rather than rely on
obtaining finance from the parent companies. In a few cases,
the head offices have requested the repayment of outstanding
debts by the subsidiaries. This, of course, has placed an un-
expected burden on the local banks; and, to a certain extent has
nullified the efforts of the authorities in the United Kingdom to
restrict the money supply. Our interests in this regard are con-
flicting because while we have everything to gain by the
measures taken to stabilise the pound and we benefit also by the
high interest yield on our London assets, any impediment to the
flow of capital outwards from London has adverse effects on the
country's balance of payments.

30. It is generally accepted that if the sterling system, as we
know it, is to function satisfactorily, the outflow of capital from
London should be maintained and, if possible, substantially
increased. This country which has since the Second World War
attracted something of the order of £250 million of British
capital has little to complain about. But, with respect, there is
one aspect of the London capital market on which I feel that I
should comment, namely, the Capital Issues Committee. In
existing circumstances, it is obvious that some form of regula-
tory machinery is needed, but, ideally, the flow of capital
from the hub towards the outlying parts of the sterling area
should be governed mainly by ordinary market forces. As far
as circumstances permit, therefore, I would favour a gradual
reduction of the scope of the Capital Issues Committee; and,
ultimately, its total abolition. I need hardly add that I strongly
disfavour certain proposals which have been made recently in
Britain for the extension of controls to embrace all movements
of capital to sterling countries. Nothing could, I believe, be
better calculated to bring about the speedy dissolution of the
system than proposals of this kind.

31. It has been suggested also that the machinery of the
sterling system should be formalised. While I would be in
favour of any proposals for improving the existing procedures
for consultation between members, from a purely central bank
point of view, I feel I ought to say that our present relationships
with the Bank of England are all that could be desired. More-

over, I do not believe that the mere setting up of a sterling area secretariat, as has been proposed in certain quarters, would necessarily be an improvement on the present arrangements. Indeed, in certain circumstances it might be positively harmful.

Reserve Bank of India

37. A substantial proportion of India's trade is with the sterling countries, nearly 54 per cent of her total exports and about 45 per cent of her imports. Traditionally, an appreciable volume of India's non-sterling transactions has also been settled in sterling. The proportion of her trade which is invoiced in sterling is on an average almost two-thirds. Another 20 per cent of the trade is invoiced in rupees, leaving only about 13 per cent of the total trade for which payment is made or received in non-sterling currencies, mainly the U.S. and Canadian dollars. Given convertibility of sterling for members of the area, the precise manner of invoicing becomes of secondary importance. It is for this reason that despite the difficulties which sterling had to face in the post-war period, there has not been a significant increase in the quantum of dollar invoicing. Structurally the main change in India's foreign trade has been the greater dependence on non-sterling sources of supply, particularly Western Europe. In 1951–52 the O.E.E.C. countries supplied 11 per cent of India's total imports: in 1957–58 the proportion had risen to as much as 25 per cent.

38. Despite the increase in total imports and the shift towards non-sterling sources, India has been able to meet her international obligations fully. In the immediate post-war years the United Kingdom Government had imposed, in terms of the Indo-United Kingdom Financial Agreement of 1947, limitations on the total amount of the accumulated sterling balances that could be drawn upon during a year and the amount that could be spent in the dollar area. Subsequently, as the balance of payments of the United Kingdom improved, larger amounts were released and the limitations on their use for making payments in the dollar area came gradually to be removed. There is no longer any restriction on the use of the sterling balances for

global payments apart from what India herself may wish to impose with a view to the maintenance of a reserve. We believe that the convertibility of sterling holdings, subject to the self-restraint autonomously exercised by member countries with due regard to their individual situation as well as the position of the general reserves of the system, is the most important advantage which India and other members of the sterling area enjoy. As far as India's recourse to the sterling area dollar pool is concerned, over the decade 1948 to 1957, this country made a net contribution of $154 million, inclusive of India's drawings from the International Monetary Fund and receipt of aid and loans from the dollar area. This figure, however, does not give a complete account of the actual impact of India's external transactions on the sterling area's gold and dollar reserves. Membership of the sterling area has enabled India to make payments in sterling to the E.P.U. countries which had to be met partly in dollars. In general the pooling of reserves is a convenient feature of the sterling system which enables the surpluses and deficits of different parts of the area to offset one another as well as the surpluses and deficits of one member country at different times to be averaged out with relatively moderate changes in the aggregate level of reserves. Members of the system thus obtain the advantage of convertibility of their reserves into an international currency of wide usage and the consequent facility of conducting international trade and transactions on a multi-lateral basis.

39. On the other hand, there has been a loss of real purchasing power suffered by the reserves consequent on the devaluation of sterling in 1949. International reserves are not only a predominantly liquid means of payment but they also represent a store of value. The United Kingdom Government's decision to devalue sterling by 30 per cent in terms of the U.S. dollar in September 1949 marked down the value of India's sterling balances by the same amount in terms of gold and dollars. In the circumstances in which the United Kingdom found herself after the war, devaluation was presumably inevitable. But in our opinion which we believe to be the opinion of United Kingdom authorities as well, a pound of stable value is indis-

pensable for the smooth and efficient working of the sterling system.

40. A factor which contributed to the strengthening of the sterling area system was the easy accessibility to the London capital market enjoyed by member countries. Although there has been no restriction on the outflow of capital from the United Kingdom to the sterling area countries, the capital has not always moved in sufficient amounts for meeting genuine demands for development. The extent to which the United Kingdom can continue to act as banker of the sterling system would depend on its capacity to continue to perform its traditional role of supplier of long-term capital to the sterling area countries.

41. We are inclined to consider that the institution of more formal arrangements than now exist for regulating the essential features of the sterling system will be open to difficulties and the present informal arrangements are generally adequate for the purpose, having regard to the somewhat flexible character of the arrangements and the importance of safeguarding the right of individual decision of member countries on vital questions. But there would be some undoubted advantage in organising more frequent discussions on the working of monetary policies, exchange controls and related questions of trade and economic policy among member countries of the sterling system. Perhaps the occasion of annual meetings of the International Bank and the International Monetary Fund could be availed of more systematically than it has been hitherto, for this purpose.

CENTRAL BANK OF CEYLON

16. Being a country whose external trade is financed mainly in sterling and whose international reserves are also held mainly in sterling, Ceylon has no desire to sever its connection with the sterling area. She has therefore kept the flow of payments between her and the other members of the area as free and unrestricted as possible, and maintained a large degree of freedom of transfer of funds within the area, such few restrictions as are imposed being due to balance of payments difficulties. Ceylon

considers it an advantage to remain within the area, though one benefit to her from such membership has recently diminished, namely, that of free access to the London money and capital markets, since the United Kingdom is unable in present circumstances to supply capital on any large scale. At this very moment, the Ceylon Government is obliged to seek external loans in America rather than in the United Kingdom. Ceylon, in accordance with the conventions of the area, has limited her dollar expenditure, endeavoured to increase her dollar earnings, and contributed a substantial proportion of her net dollar accruals to the Central Reserves of the area. The principle of Ceylon holding an 'independent' dollar reserve has been accepted but consultations have taken place with a view to limiting the size of this reserve. The position, as now understood by Ceylon, is that she is free to dispose of her net accruals of dollars as desired, but her wish will in normal circumstances be to make an appreciable contribution of such accruals to the Central Reserves of the area. As a member of the area, she recognises that she should do her best to strengthen the position and value of sterling as a world currency. Unilateral action on the part of a member, as for example, the United Kingdom, twice taken since the war—once in respect of devaluation of the pound, and more recently in freezing Egypt's sterling—is to be deprecated as tending to shake confidence in the availability of sterling for international use. A stronger sense of the need for internal discipline among all members must prevail if unevenness in the sharing of benefits and burdens is to be avoided, and while this forms the underlying sentiment behind the periodical conferences that take place at various levels it cannot be set forth in terms of an enforceable regulation.

(iv) *The Future of the Sterling Area*

(*a*) Statement by the Chancellor of the Exchequer in House of Commons. (Source: *Hansard*, 15 April 1958, cols. 51–52)

Before I come on to our future policies, I want to say a few words about sterling and the sterling area. I recalled earlier the

Government's declaration that the strength of sterling remained the primary objective of our economic policy. By that I mean not only a stable value for the pound at home and abroad, I mean the successful working of the sterling area system.

These sterling area arrangements are extremely flexible. The essential features are the use of sterling as a reserve currency by the other countries in the area, the freedom of capital movements from this country to the rest of the sterling area, and the wide and largely unrestricted use of sterling not only by these countries but by many others for trading purposes. These arrangements have proved of immense value in recent years, not only to us but to the whole sterling and non-sterling world.

Unless sterling is strong it cannot continue to be the currency which finances a large part of the world's trade. There is no other currency in a position to take its place; nor could one quickly be developed. This is a matter not only of experience, but also of banking connections abroad and the facilities of the City of London. No country is more dependent on international trade than ours; none would suffer more from the lack of a medium for financing it.

It seems rather a pity, therefore, that in recent months voices should have been heard questioning the value of the system and to suggest that in some unspecified way it might be wound up or that it should at least be drastically altered. Admittedly our reserves are not as big as we should like, particularly in relation to our liabilities. This is in part the aftermath of war. But this insufficiency can be exaggerated. The liabilities look big on paper. But we should remember that a large part of them are held for long-term purposes. Provided that confidence in sterling is maintained, only a relatively small proportion will have to be met in the immediate future.

It is also the case that at the present time, temporarily and for reasons partly outside their control, a number of sterling area countries are having to draw down their balances. This puts a strain on the reserves and limits the freedom of our domestic action. To a large extent, however, the run down in their balances is due to a change in the terms of trade. This same change in the terms of trade makes it easier for us to meet the strain.

Moreover, the fact that sterling area countries can draw down their balances in bad times, just as they build them up in good times, is a most useful contribution to world liquidity. In present circumstances this is likely to prove of great value as a cushion against the effects of diminishing income in the primary producing countries which hold their reserves in sterling.

I hope, therefore, that we shall neither exaggerate the difficulties that come from our position as the banker of the sterling area, nor underestimate its value to us. In a world where liquid reserves in other forms are all too scarce, sterling and the sterling area are indispensable to the smooth functioning of a large part of the world's trade, as well as to the unity and strength of the Commonwealth. We do not intend to tamper with this system, which is working well. On the contrary, our purpose is that it shall be preserved and developed, that confidence in its viability should be fortified, and that we shall be able to move gradually towards still wider freedom and, as opportunity offers, make yet greater contributions to Commonwealth development.

This all means that we must conduct our own finances with a special caution in difficult times. It requires, too, that we should maintain close and continuous consultation with our sterling area partners.

(b) *Conclusions of the Radcliffe Committee*
(Report, paragraphs 657–63)

657. Although there have been occasions when the functioning of the sterling area has thrown an added strain on the reserves and when the capital requirements of the area have added to the total load on the reserves of the United Kingdom, we are satisfied that it is in the interest of this country to maintain existing arrangements. We do not think it possible to dissociate these arrangements either from the long-standing trading relationships that lie behind them or from the political and other links by which most of the members of the area are joined in the Commonwealth. What is decisive in our view, is the general

harmony of interest between the United Kingdom economy and that of the rest of the sterling area, and the mutual convenience of free multilateral trading relationships within the area.

658. This does not imply that, in a world of full convertibility of currencies, these relationships should be confined to the sterling area, nor that the members of the area should maintain an attitude of exclusiveness towards other countries. Convertibility would inevitably tend to weaken some of the links between the members and remove inhibitions about running a deficit with non-sterling countries; but it does not appear to us that it would alter anything fundamental in the functioning of the area. On the other hand we do not rule out the possibility that the relationships might have to become closer and more restrictive if the world economy were again to become seriously out of balance.

659. We do not rest these conclusions on any calculations submitted to us to show the commercial value of the use of sterling as an international currency. These calculations demonstrate that the invisible earnings of what is loosely described as 'the City' are substantial, and may reach a total of about £125 million. But they do not demonstrate that these earnings would be perceptibly less if the settlements that now take place in sterling came to be made, under a different system of payments, in some international currency such as 'bancor'. These earnings and the international use of sterling are not so much effect and cause as the common outcome of the same set of circumstances: the 19th-century development of the non-European world round a largely British core and the growth of institutions, business connections and trade centring on London.

660. Various criticisms have been made to us of sterling area arrangements, and proposals have been made for modifying or superseding them. No one has suggested to us that the United Kingdom could or should terminate the sterling area by unilateral action or repudiate her liabilities to holders of sterling, and we have naturally excluded any such idea. Some witnesses have suggested that it might be possible to freeze existing balances, or limit the rate of withdrawal by agreement with the holders; but we see no likelihood of action along those lines.

661. Other members of the sterling area might wish to reconsider their position if action on the part of the United Kingdom seriously limited the advantages which they expect to derive from the use of sterling. In particular, they would be strongly influenced by action on the part of the United Kingdom cutting them off from access to United Kingdom capital. Sterling area countries may not have been able to raise all the capital that they would have liked on the United Kingdom capital market since the war, but the United Kingdom has been their chief overseas source of capital.

662. We regard the right course of action as one calculated to add to reserves or reduce liabilities out of a current surplus sufficiently large to leave room also for long-term investment abroad. We do not suggest that the improvement in reserves and liabilities should be brought about precipitately. Repayment of sterling balances, so far as they constitute the central reserves of other countries or the working balances of overseas commercial banks, would tend to reduce the liquidity of overseas monetary systems. If sterling outgoings were restricted in order to force these countries to draw on their sterling resources, some of them might be faced with a sterling shortage and a general contraction of activity would be precipitated in a group of countries which includes some of the United Kingdom's principal export markets. The same kind of situation might arise in other markets if the United Kingdom tried to restrict imports in order to add to the reserves. Quite apart from the fact that such action would be inappropriate in a period of trade recession, efforts by the United Kingdom to improve her own liquidity are bound to reduce the liquidity of other countries and aggravate any shortage of international liquidity. We should therefore refrain from seizing too eagerly on the opportunity of extinguishing short-term debts as a means of strengthening, if only temporarily, the pound sterling.

663. So long as there is no special danger of a general shortage of international liquidity, an increase in reserves should, in our view, have priority. No doubt the United Kingdom has not much freedom of choice as to whether to strengthen her position by increasing reserves or reducing liabilities; the decision is

largely governed by the willingness of other countries to hold sterling. An increase in reserves, however, marks more unambiguously than a decline in sterling balances a strengthening of the position of sterling and would be so interpreted by financial opinion. If the decline were in the balances of sterling countries it would do little to reinforce the liquidity of the sterling area as a whole, although it would improve the position of the United Kingdom. What the United Kingdom can do to add to her reserves depends, however, on the state of international liquidity, and this also has a direct bearing on the reserves which she requires.

APPENDIX

An Estimate of the United Kingdom's Overseas Assets and Liabilities

(Note: This estimate was originally published in the *Westminster Bank Review* for August 1960. It is reproduced here as originally published except for the omission of two concluding paragraphs.)

In the early post-war years no survey of the United Kingdom economy was complete without reference to wartime losses of overseas investments and the new burden of external debt: in the belief that the country had been transformed 'from the world's greatest creditor into the world's greatest debtor', these factors were given much weight as an explanation of current difficulties. Later, it was not unusual for commentators to criticize the post-war performance of the economy in relation to exports of capital ('perhaps the most disappointing part of its history') and as recently as 1958 the Radcliffe Committee was told that it was doubtful whether the United Kingdom was a creditor or a debtor.

Data now available should help to rectify such impressions. Official estimates put gross capital exports since the war at more than £4,000 million: as the total of all United Kingdom overseas investment in 1939 was of the order of £4,500 million (accumulated during a period of about 100 years), the post-war record in fact seems outstanding. It also implies that the United Kingdom may have regained its former status as a creditor country. This article sets out the evidence on the latter point.

Some years ago the present writer had occasion to put forward rough estimates of the net debtor position in 1950. On the basis of the material then available, it was suggested[1] that on capital account the United Kingdom was a net debtor to the extent of some £800 million, with a reservation to the effect that this debit might be reduced if not all the sterling balances represented external liabilities. The estimate contrasted with a net credit of some £4,000 million before the war. The details of the computation need not be reworked here (they are on record) but in the light of more recent information it now seems justifiable to reduce the debit for the

[1] In *The Sterling Area* (Macmillan, 1952).

earlier post-war years to approximately £500 million, mainly on the ground that the United Kingdom's liabilities were rather over-estimated. Even at the time it was noted that the debit was not un-duly large in relation to the total balance of payments, was relatively much less onerous than that borne by many debtor countries before the war, and in absolute terms was rather less than the current net indebtedness of Canada.

The exact amount of the debit of ten years ago is now a matter of minor importance and need not be further considered. The task here is to assess the probable present position. Three main categories of overseas assets and liabilities call for examination. In the first place there is the net total for long-term private investment. Secondly, there is the net amount due as Government debt. Finally, there is the balance between short-term liabilities and the reserves of inter-national currency held against them. Each of these groups will be reviewed in turn.

The computation can start from the pre-war estimate of £4,500 million for private investment overseas. As wartime sales amounted to £1,100 million, the 1945 total (with only slight allowance for a natural increase through reinvestment) may provisionally be put at £3,500 million. During the next few years this was further reduced as a result of diverse factors: in particular there were sales in South America and losses in China as well as some repatriation of public debt and private investment from Commonwealth countries. In the aggregate the post-war erosion seems to have amounted to rather more than £500 million.

For the period 1946–57 there are official estimates (reproduced in the Report of the Radcliffe Committee) which show gross capital exports on private account at over £3,200 million: with a further £600 million for 1958–59, the post-war increment is nearly £4,000 million. On that basis it would be reasonable to assign a figure of about £7,000 million for the present value of private investment overseas: this in monetary terms is well above the pre-war total.

Certain qualifications are, however, needed. Of major importance is the fact that the Radcliffe Committee's estimates are 'seriously incomplete', primarily because investment from retained profits is covered only in part: the omission is significant since post-war investment has been effected largely through reinvestment (in several countries one-third or more of the capital inflow has accrued in this way). Moreover, the figure suggested makes no provision for any increase in the value of the pre-war investment occasioned by inflation, full employment or similar causes: with half the 1939 total in equities and the equity index three times as high as twenty years ago, it is clear that a very large correction should be made under this head. Finally, a further correction would be necessary to take account of the 1949 devaluation, which increased the sterling value of dollar holdings. Making allowance for all these factors, it seems proper to adopt the figure of £7,000 million only as a minimum, with the proviso that the true total might well be appreciably greater.

Foreign investment in the United Kingdom must be deducted from this credit. Here again estimation is necessary at the outset since there are no official figures to use as a base. In 1950 the United States had direct investments in the United Kingdom amounting to £300 million; nationals of the Irish Republic owned securities worth perhaps half as much (apart from Government and banking funds, which would be included in the sterling balances). There is no evidence that any other country owned substantial long-term assets, though no doubt the aggregate for Commonwealth and European countries might be quite considerable. On the whole it would probably be an overstatement to put the total at £1,000 million in 1950. Subsequently, however, there was a large inflow, mainly from the United States: during the years 1952–58 this amounted to no less than £900 million. For present purposes it seems safe to take a figure of well under £2,000 million.

The net total for private investment must therefore be derived from a credit of over £7,000 million and a debit of less than £2,000 million: perhaps a balance can be struck at £5,500 million. This would still appear to be a conservative estimate.

The position on Government account can be readily stated. The external debt of the United Kingdom (nearly all loans from the United States and Canada) was £2,173 million at the end of 1957, while loans due from other Governments totalled £394 million: allowing for subsequent repayments and some further lending by the United Kingdom, the net debit would now be under £1,500 million. Some additional items in this group may be mentioned. On the credit side they would include certain assets other than loans (such as the investments of the Colonial Development Corporation, holdings in the International Bank, etc.) while on the other hand there is still an outstanding liability due to the International Monetary Fund. These items, however, can be largely offset against each other, leaving the net total at approximately £1,500 million.

The figures for the first and second of the three groups specified earlier may now be consolidated. When the debit on Government account is charged against the estimated credit for private investment, the credit balance comes out at £4,000 million.

There remains the third group of international assets and liabilities. Here there are official figures for both sides of the account but they cannot be accepted at face values since the sterling balances are over-stated and the reserves of international currency under-stated. In the most general terms the lack of any proper basis for comparison between the two is largely due to the fact that the coverage of the figures is much wider for the sterling balances than for the international reserves. The difference between them, therefore, yields an unduly adverse result.

An appropriate adjustment can be made to the figures for the reserves. The Radcliffe Committee noted that the published data referred only to the liquid reserves under the immediate control of the authorities: they thus exclude balances held abroad by United Kingdom banking, insurance and commercial concerns (at the end of 1958 the dollar element in these balances was about £300 million). It also seems right to include the United Kingdom subscriptions to the International Monetary Fund paid in gold and dollars (£150 million), which were originally taken from the reserves and can be drawn on at any time. With these additions the official figure (£1,000 million) may be raised to approximately £1,500 million.

It is more difficult to arrive at a realistic valuation of the sterling balances. In this case, too, the misleading presentation of the figures evoked comment from the Radcliffe Committee, who pointed out that the official total did not represent a net liability as the balances were recorded gross, and these liabilities include some to which there are counterparts in the form of liabilities to the United Kingdom: on a true basis the working balances in foreign currencies held by United Kingdom trading and financial concerns (other than the dollar balances already accounted for) should be set off against the London deposits of overseas banks, while the net position on external commercial credit should also be brought into the reckoning. The Committee expressed the view that if these assets were included, the net liabilities of the United Kingdom would be much lower than appears from the published figures.

Although there is no estimate of the extent to which the official totals are over-stated, there is evidence to suggest that it may be very considerable. The Radcliffe Committee itself put the working balances of United Kingdom firms at nearly £300 million for the United States alone; official returns for South Africa show that foreign trade liabilities and other short-term obligations due to the United Kingdom exceeded £100 million in 1956; the Irish bank returns also show liabilities payable in the United Kingdom at over £100 million. The samples are for three countries only but can be used to gauge the possible margin of error: in view of the world-wide range of British commercial and banking interests, the aggregate of these items must be enormous. If in fact the published totals exclude such assets (or a large proportion thereof) it seems clear that a drastic correction should be made to give the net liability.

This is not the only correction needed, since the figures are suspect for another reason also. It is known that the sterling balances of the Colonies (which account for about one-third of the total) over-state very considerably the indebtedness of the United Kingdom. The category comprises a number of different elements and although the term 'colonial sterling balances' is used to cover all assets held in London on colonial account, these assets are in fact to a large extent owned by the United Kingdom and not by colonial residents. This qualification applies especially to the items which make up the greater part of the total, viz. banking funds and currency reserves. In both cases the balances are (probably for the most part) only nominal liabilities since the sterling used as currency backing comes from the London offices of banks (generally British-owned) with branches in the colonies, while the banking funds are the London accounts of such branches.

The foregoing analysis suggests that the sterling balances as now presented grossly inflate United Kingdom liabilities. But by how much? Although in the present context it would be wrong to accept the published total (£3,350 million after deduction of acceptances), it seems impracticable to revise it except on some arbitrary basis. Limiting the possibilities to round figures, it might well be concluded, on the evidence reviewed above that £3,000 million would still be an over-statement and that £2,500 million would be nearer the mark. Here the lesser value will be taken. It cannot be justified in detail but that applies also to the official figures; moreover, they can be proved to be much too large while this cannot be proved to be much too small.

Valued as stated, the sterling balances may be set against the adjusted figure for the international reserves: this gives an estimated debit of £1,000 million. Those who prefer to assign a higher value to the liabilities can amend the estimate accordingly.

It is now possible to combine the data for the three groups considered and relate the final total to comparable estimates for earlier years. The evidence is summarised in the following table, which exhibits variations in the international debtor/creditor status of the United Kingdom over a twenty-year period. It does not purport to be a definitive statement: that would necessitate a more searching scrutiny of the items involved, which would in turn require fuller information than is at present available. But although a high degree of accuracy cannot be imputed to the component parts, there seems little reason to doubt the general validity of the results.

If these estimates prove well-founded, there has clearly been a quick recovery in recent years: although the pre-war position may not yet have been fully restored, rapid progress has been made towards that objective. The current rate of progress is relevant in this context since net overseas investment is running at £200 million per annum and there is a continuing reduction of the dollar debt. It should accordingly be possible, on present prospects, to regain the pre-war figure very shortly, even without any change in the relationship between the sterling balances and the international reserves: an improvement in that sector would, of course, accelerate the process.

United Kingdom: Overseas Assets and Liabilities

(£ million)

	Net Long-term Investment	*Net Government Indebtedness*	*Net Short-term Liabilities*	*Total*
1939	4,000	(a)	(b)	4,000
1949	3,000	—1,900	—1,600 (c)	—500
1959	5,500	—1,500	—1,000 (c)	3,000

(a) Debts arising out of World War I omitted
(b) Sterling liabilities approximately offset by official reserves (unadjusted in both cases)
(c) Official figures adjusted as explained in text.

INDEX

INDEX

PRINTED IN GREAT BRITAIN
BY ROBERT MACLEHOSE AND CO. LTD
THE UNIVERSITY PRESS, GLASGOW